MORALITY AND POLITICS
IN MODERN EUROPE

Selected Writings of Michael Oakeshott

General editors:

Shirley Robin Letwin
Timothy Fuller

Also available:
The Voice of Liberal Learning: Michael Oakeshott on Education
(introduced and edited by Timothy Fuller)

Religion, Politics and the Moral Life (introduced and edited by
Timothy Fuller)

MORALITY AND POLITICS IN MODERN EUROPE

THE HARVARD LECTURES

Michael Oakeshott

Edited by Shirley Robin Letwin

With an Introduction by Kenneth Minogue

YALE UNIVERSITY PRESS
NEW HAVEN AND LONDON 1993

Set in Linotron Baskerville by Best-set Typesetter Ltd., Hong Kong
Printed and bound in Great Britain by Bath Press, Avon

Library of Congress Cataloging-in-Publication Data

Oakeshott, Michael Joseph, 1901–
    Morality and politics in modern Europe: the Harvard lectures /
Michael Oakeshott; edited by Shirley Robin Letwin.
        p.   cm.
    Lectures delivered 1958.
    Includes index.
    ISBN 0–300–05644–3
    1. Political ethics.   2. Individualism.   3. Collectivism.
    4. Europe—Politics and government.   I. Letwin, Shirley Robin.
    II. Title.
    JA79.018   1993
    320.5′094—dc20   93-24981
                                                                        CIP

A catalogue record for this book is available from the British Library.

CONTENTS

INTRODUCTION

Kenneth Minogue

Michael Oakeshott gave these lectures at Harvard in April 1958, and they may be considered, in the first place, as an event. He had been invited to stand in for Karl Friedrich, and he made a striking contrast with his predecessor. Instead of a venerable professor, students encountered a diffident figure in a green corduroy jacket and a string tie. His captivated audience stayed with him to the end of the series; indeed, he was often to be found talking to undergraduates after midnight, sitting cross-legged on the floor in Lowell House where he was staying.

Oakeshott came, of course, with a reputation, largely nurtured at that time by the *Cambridge Journal* which he had edited (in his usual economical way – with no more help than one part-time secretary) and in which many of the essays had appeared which were later published in *Rationalism in Politics*.[1] He was then in his fifties, and had held the chair of Political Science at the London School of Economics since 1951. It should be added that wherever he taught, he always remained in manner a Cambridge man. One of his tasks at the School was to give thirty lectures on the history of political thought.

---

[1] *Rationalism in Politics* was published in 1962, but this edition has been superseded by Timothy Fuller's 1992 Liberty Press edition, which includes previously unpublished essays, including (an essay relevant in its content to these lectures) 'The Masses in Representative Democracy'. I once asked Oakeshott why he had omitted this essay from the original edition. 'I just forgot,' he replied.

One might have expected that those lectures and the ones presented here would cover the same ground. In fact, there is very little in common between them. The reason is that Oakeshott recognized every new task as an opportunity to rethink the fundamentals of what he was doing. And that is what he did when he came to Harvard.

Lecturing on the history of political thought is widely recognised as the academic equivalent of a high-wire act. Collapse into irrelevant digression, misleading taxonomy, misjudgements of detail and sheer error threaten at every turn. In recent decades, the whole field has been enriched not only by the wealth of specific studies of writers and themes, but also by extensive controversy between differing schools of thought at war over methodology. Text, context, intention, language, paradigm and many other conceptions have been fought over in the attempt to arrive at a correct method for recapturing the significance of past thinkers, and the result has certainly been a great increase in our understanding. The very success of this work, however, has only been to emphasize that the larger the scale in which the historian of ideas works, the more likely he is to fail.

Oakeshott's inclination was to reject methodological formulae and to rely upon a philosophical self-consciousness about the precise relevance of the questions being asked and answered. For one thing, the expression 'political thought' referred to a great miscellany of very different inquiries made in different contexts and with a variety of purposes in mind. The very model of uncritical miscellany in this field was recognized to be Sabine's famous textbook which Oakeshott yet also considered as a bravura performance in its own way. When he was dealing with the entire history of political thought from the Greeks to the present, as at LSE, Oakeshott had sometimes used the 'plot' sketched out in his famous introduction to *Leviathan*. There he had distinguished two almost immemorial traditions of political understanding. The first of these (Plato's *Republic* being its masterpiece) considered civil association in terms of the ideas of reason and nature; the second (brilliantly represented by Hobbes) emphasized those of will and artifice. These points of orientation allowed him to detect emerging in the modern world a third tradition in which the state was understood to be historically specific. It was an association of those 'whom choice or change had brought together' and which had over time evolved a character of its own which could not be assimilated either to rationality or to will. He sometimes called this tradition that of historical coherence. Hegel and Burke were, in different idioms, notable exponents of it.

It was further characteristic of Oakeshott's way of approaching the subject to clarify the questions being asked in different kinds of political writing. Indeed, the word 'clarification' has become rather too commonplace to express quite the force of what he tried to do: perhaps we should invent some new term such as 'unmuddling'. He recognized the state (like the *polis* and the *civitas*) as a form of association, and the basic questions concerning politics as being concerned with two issues: firstly, what is the constitution of the authority of the association? Secondly, what are the activities which states pursue, and ought to pursue? Even this elementary apparatus was sufficient to allow him to diagnose one not uncommon muddle to be found in some political thinkers. It consists in believing that any particular constitution of government would entail some specific type of activity – as when Kant approved of a republican constitution because he thought that it would automatically pursue peace, or Paine a democratic one because he thought democracies would keep down the cost of government.

Oakeshott had no need of contemporary methodology to be persuaded that politics must be understood in terms of its context. There are, however, many things which might count as context, even if one avoids the error of turning the context into a theory, as C.B. Macpherson notably did in seeing Hobbes in terms of a capitalist system supposedly on the rise in the seventeenth century. In his LSE lectures, Oakeshott's procedure was to begin with an account of what today would be called the 'political culture' of each of the four 'experiences' to which the thinkers of Western politics belonged. Those experiences were Greek, Roman, medieval, and modern. One could learn a great deal from looking at the vocabulary in which the peoples of those days expressed themselves. It was only on the basis of a consideration of these cultures that he proceeded to give an account of more abstract levels of thought. It was a procedure which sometimes led to eccentric judgements – for example, treating Aristotle before Plato on the ground that he was closer to the experience of the Greeks. But pedagogically it was marvellously successful.

In the Harvard lectures that follow, Oakeshott is concerned only with modern political thought from the sixteenth century onwards. Even so, he is typically reflective about the fact that this is an enterprise in the mode of history, and he begins with some reflections which will be recognized as characteristic by those familiar with *On History and Other Essays*. The reader will soon discover that for Oakeshott, engaging in any intellectual activity was to be profoundly self-reflective. The result is that these lectures are almost evenly balanced between historical and philosophical material.

Context, we have noted, can be many things. In considering the history of modern thought on this scale, Oakeshott decided that the relevant context was to be found not in social conditions or historical events but in the changing moral beliefs of Europeans. The story he has to tell is necessarily what he elsewhere calls an 'abridgement' and it goes as follows. Europe inherited from the middle ages what he calls a 'morality of communal ties'. In some parts of Europe, this morality survived until comparatively recent times, but from the sixteenth century onwards, a 'morality of individuality' came steadily to supersede it. A morality of individuality appears when individuals come to value and practice the making of their own decisions about their own beliefs, activities and occupations, to the extent that this is compatible with similar conduct on the part of others; and further it involves approving of this way of conducting one's life as the only one appropriate to human beings. (p. 32.) It will already be clear from my abridgement of an abridgement that we have here a carefully worked out version of the familiar story of modernity, a story sometimes told in terms of the bourgeoisie, sometimes of the inner-directed man, or the Protestant ethic, as well as in other forms. Emblematic writers such as Montaigne and moral theorists such as Kant would be completely misunderstood, or seem merely eccentric, unless seen within this context. It is this morality which, bearing increasingly on the activities of government, generated the sequence of thinkers whom Oakeshott groups as elaborating the political theory of individualism – thinkers such as Locke, Paine, Burke and (with reservations) Mill.

Individualism was certainly the most striking moral innovation of modern times, but it was an adventure on which many Europeans did not embark. In the story as often told, European life is divided between individualists on the one hand, and those who remained rooted in communal tradition on the other. Oakeshott however takes the view that where individuality came to dominate life, it destroyed the morality of communal ties but did not always replace it. This left a large population who were 'unable or unwilling' to make choices for themselves. These peoples were the materials of what Oakeshott calls a morality of 'anti-individualism' in which ' "security" is preferred to "liberty", "solidarity" to "enterprise" and "equality" to "self-determination": every man is recognized as a debtor who owes a debt to "society" which he can never repay and which is therefore the image of his obligation to the "collectivity".'(p. 27.)

Oakeshott's view of those exhibiting this new disposition is unequivocally negative: here we have 'mass man' or what he calls 'the anti-individual'. Such a creature is moved by envy and resentment, and his main desires are to be managed by a beneficent government and to create a morality which would relieve him of the feeling of insufficiency and guilt induced in such people by the dominance of individuality. (p. 190.)

These are the people who, as political materials, provoked what Oakeshott calls the political theory of collectivism. Its founder is Francis Bacon who, early on in the story, expounded a conception of human life as the cooperative exploitation of the fruits of the earth in the service of ever more perfect prosperity, and of government as a kind of estate management. This was a form of collectivism which threw up many versions. A religious version is to be found in Calvin's Geneva. More elaborate versions of this particular kind of collectivist thought focussed on the idea of productivity and were generated by Robert Owen, Saint Simon and Marx. In treating Marx, Oakeshott is primarily concerned with the question of what it is to be a human being. The moral rather than the economic is always his central focus. This is an important contrast with thinkers such as Hayek who in some other respects take a similar viewpoint.

Oakeshott also identifies a 'distributionist' version of collectivism which emerges clearly in Babeuf and his associates, and whose central idea is that of equality of distribution of the goods of a modern society. These doctrines have become increasingly dominant in modern states and their evident tendency is to treat human beings not as individuals but as featureless resources of a productive enterprise. There is no doubt that Oakeshott finds this manner of thinking inadequate to the full potentialities of human experience.

Such is the structure of the story which Oakeshott tells of modern political thought, but it is far from exhausting the

INTRODUCTION

concerns of this extremely compressed work. Oakeshott was, for example, fascinated by different ways of understanding – what he came to call, in *On Human Conduct* 'conditional platforms of understanding'. In the third lecture of *Morality and Politics in Modern Europe* he considers one unusual way of understanding politics which he illustrates in terms of the thought of Montesquieu. It consists in the attempt to delineate the 'character' of an activity by considering the set of stable dispositions which the activity reveals over some stretch of time. A 'character' of this kind is a 'rut or channel which has been excavated by human choices' and 'which gradually chisels out its own restrictions . . .'. (p. 30.) One might in these terms explore the 'character' of some specific passage of politics – that of the French *ancien regime*, for example, or of eighteenth-century England. But in Montesquieu we find the more ambitious project of attempting to elicit the character of modern European politics as a whole. It is in these terms that Oakeshott explores the familiar tripartism found in Montesquieu of despotism, monarchy and what Oakeshott calls 'democracy'.

In a short compass, then, these lectures offer a tightly organized scheme for making sense of the history of modern political thought; one that is full of suggestive remarks about method. It also offers an account of some notable figures in that history as they appear through the net of these understandings. They reveal a good deal of Oakeshott's own philosophy. He was a perfectionist, fastidious of thought without being precious. He did not choose to publish these lectures himself but, always distrusting himself impromptu, he took good care before delivering them, to work them out in the relatively finished form here presented.

Kenneth Minogue
May, 1993

PART I

THE ACTIVITY OF GOVERNING

THE HISTORY OF POLITICAL THOUGHT

Every man's reading of past events comes to acquire, in the course of time, a certain conceptual structure. It is not a structure he merely invents and imposes upon the course of events, but one which he believes himself to have elicited from his study of events and which he uses to keep his thoughts in order. In the happiest circumstances little or nothing need be said about this conceptual structure; it need not be very elaborate, it operates unseen, and it may be left to subsequent critics to unearth and tear to tatters. But when time is brief and abridgement is unavoidable, a man may be excused if he takes a short-cut and introduces what he has to say about the course of events by giving some account of the conceptual structure his thoughts have acquired. For in doing so he will indicate (but not of course justify) the directions in which he proposes to look, the features of the landscape which he takes to be important and the connections and distinctions he has come to believe to be relevant. Consequently, I propose to begin by considering the general concepts which inform what I have to say about the history of political thought.

History is an activity in which we attempt to make past happenings intelligible to ourselves. The intelligibility sought is not that which comes from understanding events as examples of the operation of general laws or as the effects of general causes, but that which appears when particular events are seen in contexts of various dimensions. The overt actions of men take on a certain intelligibility when we recognize them as the ingredients of a disposition to behave in a certain manner, the dispositions of conduct in turn become understandable when they are recognized as the idiosyncracies of a certain human character, and the human character becomes less mysterious when we observe it, not as a general type or as a possibility, but in its place in a local context. And the process may be continued in the gradual expansion of this context in place and time. At certain points conclusions may emerge which will be convincing insofar as there are no gaps or arbitrary jumps in the construction: their warrant lies, not in any self-evident truth, but in the continuity of the process which generated them. A man's lineage may appear in his face, but we are convinced of it only when we have before us, verified at each stage, his unbroken pedigree. This manner of understanding events may leave many questions unanswered; it may only result in making things a little less mysterious than they were; and the intelligibility it imparts may be only an illusion, but at least it is a modest illusion.

As I understand it, then, the history of political thought is an attempt to give this sort of intelligibility to the thoughts that have been uttered from time to time about politics. The historian is concerned not merely with the fact that men have entertained certain thoughts, but also with the context of conditions which make these thoughts intelligible. He has to do with utterances, not as isolated pronouncements, but as the ingredients of a disposition to think in a certain manner, as creatures whose character exhibits a certain pedigree, the mystery of whose emergence is qualified by being able to detect the conditions of their generation and the place they occupy in an expanding context of circumstances.

Now, whatever an historian chooses as the centre of his interest – whether it be the Thirty Years War, or Venetian painting in the fifteenth century, or the development of modern science, or sacerdotal celebacy; whether it be an incident or a doctrine or the activities of a man – it will come to him, in the first place, embedded in what may be called a special context. That is to say, he will at once recognize a context immediately relevant to the subject of his enquiry – as we recognize, for example, the contiguous sentences of a text as immediately relevant to the interpretation of a particular sentence or expression. And the historian of political thought will recognize the activity of governing and the experience of being governed as the special and immediate context of his undertaking. For it is this activity which is being thought about by the writers he is trying to interpret. And he may expect every new turn of thought to have as its immediately relevant context (but not as its cause) some change in the manner in which this activity is being carried on. Political thinkers are not then waiting to set up a government and casting about for some way of doing this: they are men reflecting upon a current activity with a view to making it intelligible to themselves and perhaps also to modifying its current conduct.

The historian, of course, will not go far before he finds himself obliged to refer to contexts other than that with which he began. If his history of the Thirty Years War began as a history of war, it will soon be found to involve also the special contexts of diplomacy and religion. And this extension of the context by admitting other special contexts is quite inescapable if the history concerns human reflection; for in making intelligible any department of the world, men have always used concepts and analogies drawn from other sources. The direction of religious and scientific thought has often been guided by analogies drawn from political activity; political reflection has been continuously conditioned by analogies drawn from biology, physiology, medicine, physics, war, religion, the conduct of business and the activity of the artist; our understanding of government cannot be, and never has been, insulated from our understanding of religion, art and the natural world. And the historian of political reflection will get nowhere unless he recognizes this. Nevertheless, in trying to make intelligible the utterances of writers on politics, his first business must be to relate them to their immediate context: the activity of governing and the experience of being governed.

But, if the immediate context of the literature of political reflection is the activity of governing and the experience of being governed, this context requires particularization. What a writer on politics has before him, what he is reflecting upon, is not this activity and this experience in general, but the particular idioms of government and politics which belong to his world. That is to say, the context we require to have before us in order to make the utterances of a political writer intelligible to ourselves is the activity of governing and experience of being governed which he himself had before him. And since our concern is with political reflection in post-medieval Europe and America, what we need to know is something about the manners and pursuits of governments since the sixteenth century. Just as the politics of fifth-century Athens will be

5

recognized as the context of Aristotle's *Politics*, and the politics of fourteenth-century Europe will be recognized as the context of Marsilius of Padua's *Defensor Pacis*, so the appropriate context of Machiavelli's political reflections is late fifteenth-century Italy, and of Hobbes's *Leviathan* the politics and government of seventeenth-century England. And even those writers who insist most strongly that they are concerned with the permanent and unchanging problems of government are in fact concerned with those problems as they appear in the circumstances of a particular time and place.

In a later lecture I propose to say something about what I believe to be the character and conditions of post-medieval European politics and government which are the particular context of the reflections of the writers we shall be considering; but before moving on from this topic, I want to put before you, not so much any conclusions I may have reached about the way in which changes in political feeling and aspiration and reasoning came about, but rather what I think the historian of such changes should be looking for.

It has been noted by Huizinga that the Middle Ages knew only what may be called applied art. The artist was recognized, and recognized himself, as a man who adorned, decorated and illustrated the activities that were afoot in a medieval community; his work was not desired and valued for its own sake but for the contribution it made to current ways of living. Art was not a means of stepping outside the routine of practical life into another world of delight and contemplation; it was used to sustain piety, to preserve the memory of notable figures and events, to make the faces of strangers known to one another, to gratify family affection and pride, to embellish the kingly office or the merchant's way of life. In short, art was recognized as an accompaniment of other activities and not as itself a self-moved activity. But by the fifteenth century, although this understanding of art did not disappear, and never has disappeared, a new attitude emerged in which works of art were recognized, not for the contribution they made to practical life, but as articles of luxury or curiosity to be admired for their own sakes. And the questions to be asked by the historian are: what provoked this change, and how did it come about? Some writers would account for it simply by postulating the appearance of a new attitude, generated by a sort of mental mutation which had no obvious connection with the outside world: people merely began to think differently about works of art, artists began to work, not as accompanists but as creators moved by a craving for beauty; and the change caught on. But an account such as this clearly fails to do what the historian should at least try to do, namely, to make the change intelligible by discerning its mediation. And what, in Huizinga's understanding of it, makes this change intelligible is that works of art, accumulated and deposited in the treasuries of princes and nobles so as to form collections, became detached from the practical uses they were designed to serve, and came to be looked at and admired in a different manner. A new taste for art was generated from a new manner of keeping and exhibiting works of art, which itself sprang not from design, but merely from a superabundance of works of art. In short, he seeks and finds in the contingencies of the outside world something to account for the new feeling for works of art that made its appearance: the art gallery, itself the product of change and circumstance and not of design, generated the new, aesthetic, as distinct from the old, practical, attitude.

Now I offer all this is an illustration of how the historian of political thought should go about his business. He will observe the appearance of new attitudes towards government, new readings of what the office of government should be, the words of a political vocabulary being given fresh meanings, current institutions and practices being understood in new manners; and, in asking himself: how did all this come about? he should seek an answer not in terms of mysterious mental mutations but in terms of modifications seen to be taking place in the manners and circumstances of human life and the conditions of government, modifications which are certainly to be understood as the products of human choices but not as the results of human design. Indeed, a large part of the literature of political reflection may be discerned as an attempt to elicit a design in, or to impose a design upon, choices which, when they were made, were in fact no more than decisions about the course to be taken in a particular emergency.

Governing is an activity which is apt to appear whenever men are associated together or even whenever, in the course of their activities, they habitually cross one another's paths. Families, clubs, factories, commercial enterprises, schools, universities, professional associations, committees and robber gangs may each be the occasion of this activity. And the same is true even of gatherings of persons (such as public meetings), so long as they are not merely ephemeral or merely fortuitous. Indeed, it may be said that no durable association of human beings is possible in the absence of this activity.

The first condition of this activity is the recognition in the association of two sets of people, rulers and ruled, a government and its subjects. No large association has ever been known literally to govern itself, or in any direct manner to appoint its own rulers. It is true that in some small and homogeneous associations (like academic or professional societies) the whole membership may be the governing body; but even where this is so, the activity of governing occurs at certain times, often in a certain place, and under rules of procedure which constitute the whole membership as, on that and similar occasions, the governing body: the distinction between rulers and ruled is intricate and oblique, but it is not abolished.

The activity itself consists in the exercise of authority by the rulers over the ruled. This authority may be of various kinds: that of the leader, of the judge or of the administrator. And it may be exercised in various manners: by exhortation, by direct command, or by making and enforcing general rules. Its result, by forbidding certain actions and by requiring others, is to determine, in part, the conduct of those who are ruled and to inculcate in them certain habits of behaviour.

In some associations this activity of ruling is understood to admit of no change: it is carried on by sacrosanct persons who owe their position to no considered constitution, and the rules and arrangements they administer are regarded as irrevocably fixed. In such associations there may be said to be an activity of governing but no 'politics'. Politics is an activity, not of governing, but of determining the manner and the matter of government, and where these are predetermined and are regarded as immune from choice or change, there is no room for 'politics'. Thus, political activity, the activity in which the composition and conduct of authority is considered, discussed, determined, criticised and modified, may be said to be an invention of Western Europe which has been spread about the world from this centre. Further, in the intensity in which it now exists, it is a comparatively modern invention. There was political activity in this sense in ancient Greece, in republican Rome, in medieval England; but it was a comparatively narrow activity, circumscribed by many hindrances which, with the disappearance of sacrosanct laws, institutions and persons and with the appearance of the belief that nothing is immune from change and everything subject to choice, have ceased to operate. Hegel was right in observing that politics in the full sense is the counterpart of the modern state whose government and public arrangements are recognized to be the product of human choices and therefore alterable at will.

Whenever government has been reflected upon and talked about, two main topics have come up for consideration:

(a) Thoughts and expectations about the constitution, composition and authorization of the governing authority.

(b) Thoughts and expectations about the engagements, pursuits or activities of the governing authority.

And it is difficult to see what could be thought or said about government which does not fall under one or other of these two heads.

Further, in respect of both these topics, reflection has, as a rule, been concerned either with elucidating and understanding the constitution or the office of government, or with determining the proper constitution or the proper office of government: it has been either descriptive or prescriptive. And on the occasions when these two attitudes have been mixed, which has not been seldom in the literature of political reflection, the result has been an unhappy but often significant muddle. For, at least at this level, inference from fact to value is unwarranted. In considering any political writer, or any passage in his writings we shall, then, do well to ask ourselves, which of these two moods is represented.

In any but the most rudimentary political literature, examples of reflection on both these topics – the constitution and the office of government – will be found. But for two reasons it is important to distinguish them. First, they are independent of one another: what we are disposed to believe or approve in respect of the authorization and constitution of government neither favours nor obstructs (much less compels or excludes) any particular disposition in respect of the pursuits of government. There have, it is true, been writers who approved of certain sorts of constitution because they believed that governments composed and authorized in this manner would automatically conduct the affairs of the association in a certain way: Kant approved of a republican constitution because he believed that a government of this kind would automatically pursue peace; and Tom Paine approved of a democratic con- · stitution because he believed that a democratic government

9

would confine its activities within the limits he approved and would be inexpensive. But both Kant and Paine were in error, not merely in respect of their empirical expectations but in respect of the logical relations between the constitutions and the pursuits of governments.

Secondly, these two topics of reflection should be distinguished because at different times and in different circumstances they are apt to occupy different places of relative importance in the literature of political thought; and on certain occasions one or other may take a place so pre-eminent as almost to exclude the other from consideration. And when this happens we should try to understand the reason for it.

In the political reflection of medieval Europe attention was mainly directed towards questions concerning the authorization of ruling authorities. And it is not surprising that this should have been so. For, whereas over the greater part of the Christian era the constitution and authorization of governments have been a subject of continuous experiment and change, the pursuits of governments have lain very little within the field of choice and have changed very little until recent times. To maintain peace and order, to guard the laws and customs of the community, when necessary to organize defence, when propitious to embark upon conquest or migration, and to deal with social and economic change when they produced an emergency – it was within this narrow round of engagements that the activity of governing was confined during the Middle Ages, in none very successful, and with resources always stretched. These are not the circumstances to breed reflection, debate or lively dispositions in respect of the pursuits of governments. And the main circumstance that prevented the activity of governing's being, or being thought proper to be, an activity of enterprise was not any abstract principle, but the conspicuous lack of power to be enterprising. For what a government does, and what it may be expected to do, and even what it may be thought proper for it to do or to attempt, are conditioned by the resources of power it already commands or plausibly hopes to command; nobody expects a government to do, or disapproves of it on account of a failure to do, what is manifestly beyond its resources. And before the sixteenth century these resources were always comparatively slender; scarcely sufficient to meet the modest expectations of subjects, with nothing to spare upon which choice could exercise itself.

But in modern times, namely during the last four hundred

years or so, the power at the disposal of governments has
steadily increased; and in response to these enlarged resources
the pursuits which governments could entertain ceased to be
confined within the relatively narrow limits of a strict convention and came to take their place in the field of enterprise.
And there has been a corresponding revolution both in what
has come to be expected from governments and in beliefs about
the proper pursuits of government. In short, a vast acces-
sion to the power enjoyed by rulers, and this power continuously incremented over a period of about four hundred years,
have given political reflection a new centre of gravity: beliefs
about the office of government have become pre-eminent, and
those concerned with the constitution and authorization of
governments are now in a subordinate position. And that this
change has not been more readily observed is due to three
circumstances.

First, beliefs about the authorization and proper constitution of governments are always important; associations in
which beliefs on these topics are vague and unsteady are associations on the verge of dissolution; it is of the utmost importance that subjects should know where their obedience lies
and that they should be convinced that authority is in proper
hands. Nevertheless, I think, so far as modern political reflection is concerned, the importance of these beliefs is derivative.
It is true that current beliefs about the proper constitution and
authorization of governments emerged slowly and were not
arrived at without extensive debate, confusion and violence,
and that this emergence spread itself conspicuously over the
face of European political history during the last four centuries;
but the significance of this process derives almost entirely
from the fact that government in respect of its pursuits had
come to enjoy a lengthened tether and could browse upon
pastures hitherto far out of its reach. Authorization mattered
more because power and activity had increased. The case
for that sort of constitution and authorization of government we call 'democracy' has been argued, whether or not
correctly, very largely on the observation of the power at the
disposal of modern governments; where it was not argued that
a democratic constitution would increase the power of government, it was argued that it is intolerable that governments
disposing of such immense power should not be democratically
constituted.

Secondly, the interest in the constitution and authorization of governments retained for a long time a fictitious pre-eminence because it was (wrongly) believed that the pursuits of governments derive directly (even necessarily) from the constitutions of governments, and that to have settled the one was to have decided the other. And in this manner was really a concern with the activities of governments disguised as a concern with the constitutions of governments.

And thirdly, this shift of interest from constitutions to activities in modern times has been concealed from us because the political vocabulary inherited by modern Europe was constructed and first used largely in relation to questions concerning the constitutions and authorization of governments, and although we have come to use many of these words and expressions (as we must, having no others) in relation to our main concern, the activity of governments, this transposition is often hidden from us because the earlier usage remains unrevoked in our minds. For example, the word 'democracy' stood originally for a government constituted and authorized in a certain manner, but it has now commonly come to be used to indicate a government active in a certain manner; and similarly the word 'freedom', which stood for a condition of human circumstance recognized to be the concomitant of government authorized in a certain manner (Rousseau, for instance, contrasts 'free' with 'monarchical' governments), now commonly refers to a condition of human circumstance springing from what a government has or has not done. And it may be observed that most of the words which in recent times have been added to our political vocabulary refer to the activities of governments, not to their constitutions.

In the history of political thought, then, it is necessary to distinguish the particular topic being reflected upon – whether it is the constitution of governments or the activities of governments. And it is my belief that during the last four hundred years there has been a gradual shift of interest from the first of these topics to the second. And also, I think it will be found that most, but not all, of the reflection and discussion that appears on the surface to be concerned with the constitution and authorization of governments is really concerned with the office and pursuits of governments.

So much for what I have called the immediate context of political thought in the modern world. This is what was before the eyes of political thinkers; it was this political experience they reflected upon.

I said earlier that it was to be expected that reflection would direct itself either on the constitution and authority of government or on the activities and office of government; and also that it might be either descriptive or prescriptive.

I want now to make another distinction, not between different topics of reflection but between different levels of reflection; for 'political thought' is a shorthand expression which covers not only thought about a variety of topics but also thought of different kinds.

If we attend to the literature of political reflection we may I think observe three main levels at which it takes place. And it is important to distinguish these different levels because, although they slide naturally into one another, and even to a small extent overlap, they are concerned with asking different sorts of questions about political experience.

There is, in the first place, the thinking that goes on when men are in the midst of political activity, or are engaged in governing – the thought that goes to the formation of a policy, for example. This may be called political thought in the service of political action. It takes place, usually, within a framework of existing political methods and institutions; and, of course, it is apt to react upon these methods and institutions, modifying them and making them more amenable for the conduct of business. And part of the task of the historian of political thought is to discover, for example, how an ancient Athenian, or a Roman, or a medieval Englishman or a seventeenth-century Frenchman, thought when he was making up his mind about the practical political problems of his day. Thucydides gives us some guidance on this question in respect of an ancient Athenian; and in more recent times we can gather from parliamentary speeches and state papers something about the processes of thought of politicians and rulers.

But in politics and government men are accustomed not only to look forward to what they want to do, but also to look back upon what they or others have done in order to discern principles and general ideas which 'explain' or justify their political desires: decisions, choices and actions. And when they do so they have moved to a new level of political thinking. The main object at this level is to make sense of political conduct by understanding it in terms of general principles. Such expressions as Liberalism, Socialism, Democracy, Imperialism,

Colonialism, Despotism, Nationalism, Sovereignty, Capitalism, Fascism, the Welfare State, Republicanism, are the products of this level of political reflection. Each of them is to be understood as a convenient shorthand expression descriptive of a certain style or manner of conducting affairs: in each a complex and intricate manner of behaving is reduced to a generality. Whether general principles of this sort really help to make the political conduct they describe intelligible is another question; and this level of political thinking is obviously very hazardous. But what the historian of political thought is concerned with is the fact that a great deal of political thinking is of this kind. And what he has to do is to try to discover how and why these general ideas came to be constructed, to understand what forms of behaviour they represent or are intended to represent, and to recognize the part that they play. Most of them are not in any proper sense 'scientific' ideas, and it is notorious what difficulties men have got into in making use of them. To abridge conduct into general principles is, then, a supremely important level of political thinking. And even at first sight it is obvious that some of these generalizations refer to the constitutions of government and others to the office or conduct of government.

But there is a third and much rarer level of political reflection. It appears when what is being attempted is neither to determine upon policy nor to make sense of political desires and actions by understanding them in the idiom of general principles but to consider the place of government and political activity on the map of human activity in general. The questions being asked at this level of thought are: what are we really doing when we are engaged in political activity? what really is this activity called 'governing'?

This level of political thinking is sometimes called 'political philosophy': it is the sort of political thinking which appears in such works as Plato's *Republic*, Spinoza's *Ethics*, Hobbes's *Leviathan* and Hegel's *Philosophie des Rechts*.

Now it is obvious that these three levels of political thinking are not entirely separable from one another. They are concerned with answering different sorts of questions, and therefore should not be confused with one another: they really are different *levels* of thinking rather than separate kinds. And further reflection might very well come to discern other levels between these.

Nevertheless, to make this sort of classification, to understand political thinking as having a general structure of this kind, serves the useful purpose of drawing our attention to the similarity between thinking about politics and government and thinking about any other human activity.

For example, it is like thinking about building houses or writing poetry or living a religious life.

To build a house, first of all, requires thought of some sort – thought in the service of the activity of building: thought about materials, the wants of customers and the abilities of workmen. And this level of thinking corresponds to the practical level of political thought which goes to the formation of policy or the construction or modification of a constitution.

But when the activity of building is well advanced and there are numerous different sorts of houses to compare with one another, we can and do begin to think at a different level – we can begin to detect and distinguish, in terms of general principles, different styles of architecture. And this corresponds to our second level of political reflection; the level in which we try to understand our desires and actions in terms of general ideas. 'The democratic style of politics' is the same sort of expression as 'the baroque style of architecture'. 'The baroque style of architecture' is the product of reflection upon buildings that have actually been constructed.

(c) But beyond this there lies a level of reflection upon building which is concerned to consider the place of the activity of building on the map of human activity in general: the attempt to discern the character of the activity itself and not merely to classify its products. And the result of this kind of reflection is a philosophy of art or architecture.

Political thinking, then, is not only concerned with different topics and is capable of taking different attitudes to the topics being considered; it also exists at different levels. And if we want to understand what a writer is saying we must try to discern:

(a) What particular topic he is concerned with: the constitution or the office of government.

(b) What his attitude is: descriptive or normative.

(c) What level he has chosen for himself: what sort of questions he is trying to answer.

2

MORALITY AND GOVERNMENT IN MODERN EUROPE

In my last lecture I said something about the immediate special context to which the historian of political thought must relate the reflections and utterances he is concerned with in order to make them intelligible. This context I described as the activity of governing and the experience of being governed. And I suggested that in considering the history of modern European political thought, this context might be narrowed to the activity of governing and the experience of being governed as it has appeared in modern Europe: this is what these political thinkers have before them, and this is what they are reflecting about.

Today I want to consider another part of the context of modern European thinking about government and politics; namely, the context of moral sentiments and beliefs.

An absolute coincidence between conduct believed to be morally wrong and conduct which is prohibited by law is not to be expected anywhere; still less is it to be expected that there will be an absolute coincidence between conduct believed to be right and conduct enjoined by law. Even where, as may be the case, there is no discord between what is enjoined or prohibited by law and what is believed to be right and wrong in human conduct, it is almost impossible for the moral beliefs of a community to be reflected in their entirety in its laws. Law and morals normally have the same centre but not the same circumference. This absence of coincidence between law and morals may in some circumstances be small, as in the case of a theocracy whose law is itself a religious law and where every crime is recognized as a sin and every sin is proscribed as a crime, or the divergence may be considerable, as in the case of an association whose members subscribe to a variety of religious and moral beliefs and yet live under one law.

Now, to have achieved a distinction between crime and sin is one of the characteristics of modern European societies. It is not a characteristic unique to these societies; elsewhere and at other times this distinction has been recognized. Nor, as we shall see later, is it an absolutely secure distinction: modern European societies have shown that they are not immune from relapse in this respect. And even in the favourable conditions of modern Europe this distinction was only slowly acquired. We owe it, in the main, to two circumstances. First, the variety of moral and religious opinion which appeared in these societies would have destroyed every vestige of social cohesion if governments had not refrained from imposing a single moral code by law. This was often attempted, particularly in small communities and in the early years of modern history. It was attempted, for example, in Calvin's Geneva, and in seventeenth-century England there were fanatics who wished to make crime coincide with sin; but neither here, nor anywhere else, did these attempts have any durable success. Secondly, the moral beliefs of European societies reflected those which had become attached to the Christian religion, and Christianity being an historic and not an indigenous religion, Christian teaching (although it often pressed its moral beliefs upon governments) always recognized a distinction between sin and crime, between what must be avoided if salvation is to be enjoyed and what might legitimately be demanded by civil law.

Nevertheless, this absence of any detailed coincidence between particular beliefs about right and wrong behaviour and what civil laws in modern European societies enjoin and forbid does not signify an absence of relation between morals and politics. Neither the constitutions of governments, nor their decisions and actions, nor the laws they promulgate have ever been immune from judgements of approval and disapproval, and they have certainly not been so in modern times. Some of these judgements, of course, concern expedience and inexpediency, wisdom and foolishness; but many of them are judgements of moral approval and disapproval relative to the constitutions and conduct of governments. Moreover, there never was a time when argument was not apt to take the form: proper conduct for human beings is such and such, therefore governments should or should not be constituted in certain manners and should or should not be active in certain matters.

All this has been so even where the activity approved for governments was not the direct enforcement of what was believed to be right for human beings.

Political reflection, then, even in modern times and in societies which recognize distinction between sin and crime, has some moral opinions as its context. But what is important, from this point of view, is not merely that we should observe the *ad hoc* moral judgements which have, remotely or directly, conditioned reflection on government and politics – for these are often erratic, inconsistent with one another and insignificant – but that we should discern the moral dispositions which have been at work. The question we must ask ourselves is: what are the moralities, or moral dispositions, which make intelligible the thoughts about government and politics that we find being uttered? And, to guard against misunderstanding, let me repeat that in asking this question we are not seeking the cause of the ideas about government and politics – we are seeking a context to which they may be referred in order to make them more intelligible.

As it appears to me, the moral opinions and beliefs current in European societies during the last five centuries or so represent three different, and to some extent mutually opposed, moralities or moral dispositions. These moralities have, I believe, been present in all these societies, though they have been present in varying degrees. And I would guess it to be true to say that every reflective individual has felt the pull of each of these moralities: they have all embedded themselves in modern European moral character which, like modern European languages, is a composite character prey to many internal stresses. They are different moralities, and their currency in these societies has unavoidably led to moral confusion and uncertainty. Moreover, since all of them use a single moral vocabulary, the words and expressions of that vocabulary have acquired a notorious ambiguity. Indeed, if I were asked: what evidence have you for the currency of three different moralities? I would answer by pointing to the different meanings attributed to the terms of our moral vocabulary. And the character of these moralities is, I think, to be elicited from the current usages of moral expressions.

The first of these moralities is the least important. So far as most modern European societies are concerned it is, in the main, a relic of the past and has only a fragmentary existence. Nevertheless it is of considerable importance for three reasons. First, until two generations ago it was current in certain parts of Europe, not as a relic of the past but as an operative moral disposition. Secondly, it has nowhere quite lost its authority or power to attract, and even where circumstances are altogether adverse to its enjoyment it has remained for many people an ideal after which they yearn. And thirdly, it has a deceptive similarity to one of the other current moralities which derives from it an undeserved *reclame*.

This morality I will call *the morality of communal ties*; its structure is familiar and I need draw your attention only to its general character. The circumstance required for its enjoyment is the existence of a community, membership of which is not a matter of choice, a community not recognized as an association composed of individuals who have made a decision to form it. The model of such a community is a family in which property is the property of the family and in which one's place, one's rights and one's duties are determined by custom, and in which loyalties are not to chosen moral principles but to persons. Such were the moral circumstances of large parts of medieval Europe in the eleventh and early twelfth centuries, and such they remained until a few generations ago in rural Russia and elsewhere. In these communities not only were ordinary activities, those concerned with getting a living, with the cultivation of the soil and the disposal of its produce, communal in character and customary in inspiration, but so also were rights and responsibilities and decisions of all sorts. Relationships and allegiances, rights and duties, sprang from one's status in the community and rarely extricated themselves from the analogy of kinship. In such circumstances, there is little or no idea of moral change or progress; indeed, a disposition in favour of change in any respect is notably absent. 'The good' is recognized as the common good of the society – of the family or of the village community. The self-knowledge of each member is the knowledge of himself as a member: he is not an individual who, for moral or prudential reasons, has chosen to surrender in some or in all respects his judgement to the authority of others; he is a person who has never enjoyed the luxury and the responsibility of private judgement. And the community is relatively small; a local community, not completely self-contained but in a very large degree so.

Now, with this morality of communal ties there goes an appropriate understanding of the constitution and office of government. Governing is, in the main, a local activity; although in each local community it may point to a larger and vaguer authority from which the local authorities derive their warrant to govern. Rulers are denoted by such expressions as *Sieur*, *Sire*, *Seignior*, all of which indicate seniority, carry the idea of superiority linked with age, and point to the analogy of kinship and family. Above these local rulers there may be a *Rex*, a king. The activity of governing is carried on in a court of law, and its character is derived from its judicial manner. Each member of the community is the suitor at a court where he goes for 'justice': governing is not an enterprising activity designed to change or better the conditions of a man's life, it is not an activity in which new interests are recognized and turned into rights; it is the administration of the laws and customs of the community. The ruler is not the bearer of an *imperium*; he is the custodian of these laws and customs, he is under an oath of loyalty to them, and his office is to maintain the 'peace' of which they are the pattern. The office of king has a superior authority, but it is an authority of the same kind as that of the inferior rulers, except that added to it was the exclusive office of military command. Indeed, in those localities where the king himself was the local ruler, in his own demesnes, his activity was little distinguished from that of a fief-holder.

So much, then, for the morality of communal ties and the understanding of government which went with it. So far as modern Europe is concerned, this morality is a relic of the past, surviving only fragmentarily; but it is important because the moralities that have succeeded to it are modifications of it, and its presence still makes itself felt within these modifications.

The process in which the morality of communal ties was modified and finally superseded was, of course, long and slow. A new moral disposition can be seen beginning to emerge from about the twelfth century, but it was not until the sixteenth century that it had appeared unmistakably over the horizon; and, even then, there remained many parts of Europe relatively unaffected until a much later time. This new moral disposition I will call the *morality of individuality*; and it is to be recognized as one of the current moralities of the modern world.

By the morality of individuality I mean, in the first place, the disposition to make choices for oneself to the maximum possible extent, choices concerning activities, occupations, beliefs, opinions, duties and responsibilities. And further, to approve of this sort of conduct – self-determined conduct – as conduct proper to a human being, and to seek the conditions in which it may be enjoyed most fully. It is in this approval – not merely on one's own account but in respect of others also – that the impulse towards individuality becomes a moral disposition. This is how human beings ought to live, and to be deprived of this exercise of individuality is recognized not only as the greatest unhappiness but also as a diminution of moral stature.

Now, the view I have put before you is that a moral disposition of this sort, or of any sort, is the concomitant of a certain condition of human circumstances. A disposition to approve of the exercise and cultivation of individuality in conduct requires for its generation a certain experience of individuality, a condition of human circumstance which is, like all such conditions, a product of choice and chance. And we may, I think, see this condition and this experience emerging in Western Europe from about the beginning of the thirteenth century. Extended opportunities of escape from the corporate and communal organizations of current medieval life offered themselves, not in a few localities only, but in varying degrees all over the continent of Europe, not in towns only (though perhaps there more than anywhere else) but even in the countryside. And all that had hitherto been governed by immemorial custom and had derived from status in a community – occupations, duties, beliefs, responsibilities – was beginning to respond to the choices of individuals. These changes were, of course, the results of human choices, but they were not shaped by men inspired by a vision of a comprehensive new way of living; they were explored (often hesitatingly) by those who saw, perhaps in one of them, an occasion which seemed to meet an immediate need. The changes proceeded blindly and piecemeal. Nevertheless, in the enjoyment of these opportunities a new idiom of conduct and character gradually emerged: the human individual, claiming to be morally sovereign over himself and engaging to live a life governed by his own choices.

The emergence of this disposition was often hindered by changes of circumstances which made the world, or some locality, temporarily unfavourable to it; and it was, of course, hindered by the current morality in which self-determination was regarded as sin, the mortal sin of *superbia*. But, in spite of these and other hindrances, it made its way, and by the sixteenth century had managed to establish itself as a moral disposition. From our point of view the Reformation may be recognized as a reflection of this disposition; religious belief and religious confession in the sixteenth century became matters often of individual choice, and among some of the reformers the salvation of a man's soul was recognized to be a matter of individual responsibility. The claims of 'conscience' were, no doubt, more often preferred than recognized, but they at least expressed a widespread conviction that in some important respects a man should be sovereign over himself. A 'privacy' hitherto unknown began to make its appearance in European life; and what the Reformers displayed in one idiom (the idiom of religious belief) the practices of commerce and industry and the policies of rulers displayed in another.

The enjoyment of these ever-growing opportunities to be an individual generated, not only an 'individual' who was more and more disposed to make use of them, but also manners of thinking in which this experience of individuality was explored and confirmed. The matchless confidence in himself and the propriety of being himself which marks Montaigne was early theorized in the writings of Descartes. A man, beyond doubt, was recognized as a *res cogitans*; and in this is found the warrant of his independent existence. For each man the starting-point of his knowledge is his own experience – not that of others or of a community. All knowledge is derived from sensation and introspection. And in this respect Descartes was followed by a long line of writers whose express design was to explain and justify this experience of individuality at the level, not only of epistomology, but also of metaphysics.

However, it was in the field of ethical theory that the clearest reflection of this experience appeared. Almost all ethical writing from the early seventeenth century begins with the hypothesis, not of a community of human beings, but of an individual human being choosing and pursuing his own directions of activity and belief. What appeared to require explanation was not the existence of these individuals, but how they could even come to have obligations to others of their kind and what were the nature of these obligations. This is unmistakable in Hobbes, the first moralist of the modern world to take candid account of the current experience of individuality. But it is clear also in Spinoza. For Locke things are good and evil only in relation to pleasure and pain, that is, in relation to the personal experience of individuals. And even those writers who, at a later stage, postulated a faculty of sympathy for others or a pre-established harmony between the desires of individuals, even those writers are concerned with the problems which this experience of individuality had thrown up. For Kant, moral goodness is attributable solely to the good will; it is in moral conduct that a man comes to know himself, for the first time, as unmistakably a sovereign individual who is free. The moral law is to acknowledge each man as an independent personality and to regard him not as a means but as an end in himself.

In short, choice working upon chance, over a period of many centuries, promoted conditions of human circumstance favourable to individuality in almost every field of human activity and enterprise. These conditions sprang from small modifications of the conditions appropriate to a morality of communal ties. And in the course of time a new morality, the morality of individuality, established itself unmistakably as one of the moral dispositions of modern Europe.

We shall have to consider later the way in which this experience of individuality, and the moral disposition which sprang from it, was reflected in the understanding of the proper constitution and proper office of government, for it is the context which serves to make intelligible a great deal of the political thinking of the last four and a half centuries. But without encroaching upon that, two things may perhaps be noticed at once. First, this moral disposition makes it appropriate to regard human societies as associations of individuals, and not as, in the strict sense, communities. And consequently one of the questions it provoked was: what ends are served by these associations? That is to say, this morality of individuality is connected with a fundamentally new direction in political thought, which, in my opinion, detracts very much from the usefulness of Gierke's twofold classification of the political theories of Western Europe into medieval and antique on the one hand, and modern theories on the other. In fact, the political reflection generated by the antique world is altogether different from the modern world. Secondly, it is worth noticing at once the intimate connection between the institution of private property and the enjoyment of individuality and the desire to explore and develop its possibilities. Where communal ties are the form and substance of moral life, private property is almost unknown (indeed, privacy in any respect has an exceedingly restricted existence); but where the pursuit and enjoyment of individuality is the image of moral conduct, private property is of the utmost significance.

The history of modern morals, however, does not end with the displacement of a morality of communal ties by a morality of individuality. There is a third important moral disposition for us to consider in relation to government and politics in modern Europe.

In a world being transformed by the aspirations and activities of those who were excited by these opportunities for individual choice, there were some people who, by circumstance or by temperament, were less ready than others to respond to its invitation; and for many the invitation to make choices for themselves came before the ability to do so, and was consequently recognized as a burden. The old certainties of belief, occupation, status, which belonged to a world organized in terms of communal ties, were being. dissolved, not only for those who had confidence in their power to make a new place for themselves in an association of individuals, but also for those who had no such confidence. The counterpart of the agricultural or industrial *entrepreneur* of the sixteenth century was the displaced labourer; the counterpart of the free thinker was the dispossessed believer. In short, the circumstances of modern Europe, even as early as the sixteenth century, bred not a single character – a man intent upon enjoying the new opportunities for individual choice – but two obliquely opposed characters: that of the individual and that of the man who could not manage to be an individual. And this other character was not a relic of a past age; he was a 'modern' character, the product of the same dissolution of communal ties as had generated the modern European individual.

In some, no doubt, this inability to respond to the invitation to be an individual provoked merely resignation; but in others it bred envy, jealousy and resentment. And in these emotions a new disposition was generated: the impulse to escape from the predicament by imposing it upon all mankind. The man frustrated by his failure to live up to the invitation of the times became a man disposed to assimilate the world to himself by deposing the individual and destroying the moral prestige he had acquired: he became the militant 'anti-individual'.

In pursuit of this task he looked round for support and he

found it in two directions. First, he looked to government to protect him from the necessity of being an individual, to make the choices on his behalf which he was unable to make for himself. And a large number of the activities of governments in the sixteenth century were devoted to the protection of those who, by circumstance or temperament, were unable to look after themselves in this world of crumbling communal ties – and, of course, have been similarly devoted ever since. But also, some of the most notable political inventions of modern Europe were designed for making choices for those who were unable or indisposed to make choices for themselves: the 'godly prince' of the sixteenth century, the 'enlightened' despot of the eighteenth century, and the 'dictators' of our own time, to mention three examples out of many. The repercussions on government and politics produced by the appearance of this 'individual' who was unable to behave as an individual have, of course, been immense, and we shall have to consider some of them later. This so-called 'mass-man' has made a great impact upon the political literature of modern Europe, but he did not, on his emergence, look only to government to support him in his adverse circumstances. He sought, in the second place, to develop a morality appropriate to his character and condition, a morality strong and convincing enough to relieve him from the feeling of guilt and inadequacy which his inability to embrace the morality of individuality provoked. I will call it the morality of collectivism.

The emergence of the morality of the 'anti-individual', a morality, namely, not of 'liberty' and 'self-determination' but of 'solidarity' and 'equality', is, of course, difficult to discern, but it is already clearly visible in the seventeenth century in those parts of Europe where the experience of individuality had been most thoroughly explored and therefore presented itself as the clearly defined enemy of the emergent 'mass-man'. The obscurity of its beginnings is due, in part, to the fact that its vocabulary was at first that of the defunct morality of communal ties; and there can be little doubt that it derived strength and plausibility from its deceptive affinity to that morality. But it was, in fact, a new moral disposition, generated in opposition to what had become the moral beginning of individuality, and calling, not for the resuscitation of an old order, but for the establishment of a new condition of human circumstance reflecting the aspirations of the 'anti-individual'.

The nucleus of this new morality was the concept of a

substantive condition of human circumstance represented as 'the common good' or 'the public good', which was understood not to be composed of the various goods that might be chosen by individuals, but to replace these. The morality of individuality had, of course, always allowed for common arrangements which, because they were understood as what each individual in pursuit of his own projects might recognize to be valuable, could properly be called 'common goods'. But for the 'anti-individual' such 'common goods' were wholly inadequate: the public good must be recognized as an entity on its own account and it must be identified with a comprehensive condition of human circumstance attracting to itself the whole of human approval. Again, while the morality of individuality had recognized 'self-love' as among the legitimate springs of human activity and sought to accommodate individuals to one another so that they might enjoy the benefits of association, the morality of collectivism pronounced 'self-love' to be evil and sought to replace it, not by the love of 'others', by 'charity' or 'benevolence' (which would have entailed a relapse into the vocabulary of individuality), but by the love of the 'collectivity' itself. No doubt there were many reminiscences here of the primitive 'solidarity' of a communal order, no doubt part of the attraction of this morality of collectivism lay in its appeal to deeply rooted moral sentiments which the morality of individuality seemed to have neglected, but in fact the 'collectivity' which was made the object of love and worship was nothing like the definite community. As Rousseau understood so well, a 'collectivity' which follows upon the emergence of an individual intent upon exploring the possibilities of individuality is wholly different from a community in which the individual has not yet emerged.

Round this nucleus of 'solidarity' revolved a constellation of appropriate subordinate moral beliefs and sentiments. From the beginning the designers of the morality of anti-individuality identified private property as evil. Indeed, privacy in any connection was recognized as an intrusion of individuality and therefore to be abrogated: an unequivocally 'public' life was perceived to be the counterpart of the 'anti-individual'. And further, it was appropriate that the morality of the 'anti-individual' should be radically equalitarian: how should the 'mass-man', whose sole distinction was his resemblance to his fellows and whose sole escape from frustration lay in the recognition of others as merely replicas of himself, approve of any divergence from exact uniformity? All must be equal and anonymous units in a 'collectivity'.

Before the end of the nineteenth century, then, a morality of 'anti-individualism' had been generated in response to the aspirations of the 'mass-man' – the man unable or indisposed to make choices for himself. In this morality 'security' is preferred to 'liberty', 'solidarity' to 'enterprise' and 'equality' to 'self-determination': every man is recognized as a debtor who owes a debt to 'society' which he can never repay and which is therefore the image of his obligation to the 'collectivity'. And attached to this morality there is an appropriate understanding of the proper constitution and office of government, which we shall later have to consider.

The view I have to put before you, then, is that the history of modern European morals displays to us two distinct and opposed moral dispositions or moralities; the morality of individualism and the morality of collectivism. I understand each of these moralities to have emerged as different modifications of an earlier morality, characteristic of medieval Europe, which I called the morality of communal ties. But, in addition to being a modification of this earlier morality, the morality of collectivism may be discerned as in some respects a reaction against the morality of individualism which had emerged and established itself in the early post-medieval period. I have had, at this stage, to be brief; but I propose to return later to examine in greater detail the character and content of each of these moralities.

Now, each of these moralities has a counterpart in an appropriate understanding of the constitution and office of government. And all the beliefs about government which have been current in modern times will be found to be logically, and often historically, connected with one or two of these moralities. Hence, these two moral dispositions may be regarded as part of the context to which the political reflection of modern Europe may be referred in order to make it intelligible. But it should be understood that I am not suggesting that these moral dispositions should be thought of as the *causes* of the dispositions which reveal themselves in the utterances of writers on politics. I do not, in fact, think that writers are apt to argue from morals to politics or from politics to morals; moral and political beliefs and sentiments usually develop in interaction with one another. Consequently they may be used to elucidate one another as text and context. And since our concern is with political reflection and belief, moral belief appears as the context. It is, moreover, in my opinion an exceedingly revealing context, more important than any other.

3

THE INVESTIGATION OF THE 'CHARACTER' OF MODERN POLITICS: MONTESQUIEU

We believe that human activity – human choices and the situations that spring from them – can be made intelligible by observing it as a sequence or succession in which situations not merely follow, but follow *from* one another, or are caused, determined or conditioned by earlier situations. And this sort of enquiry has often been used in connection with political activity; generally speaking it may be called an historical enquiry, and a good deal of the political literature which the historian of political thought has to consider is devoted to it.

There are, however, other sorts of enquiry. There is the sort of enquiry which seeks to elucidate political activity in terms of general causes, or which seeks to impose some system of classification upon the different manners of governing. What I want to do now is to bring to your notice another sort of enquiry, different from any of these, which has been used in the investigation of modern politics, and to consider the fruits which have sprung from it, or which may be expected to spring from it. I will call this sort of enquiry, the investigation of character, and the writer I want to consider in this connection is Montesquieu. The question being considered in this sort of enquiry is: what is the character of modern politics?

A man's 'character', as I shall use the word, is a balance of dispositions. This we ordinarily think we can discern when we are given the opportunity of observing and reflecting upon his conduct, his actions and his utterances, in a variety of situations. To know a man's character is to have beliefs about his dispositions and expectations, about his actions and utterances. His 'character' is not the 'cause' of his actions, it is the pattern of his conduct.

Now, the assumption here is that activity may be of two different sorts.

(a) Activity which opens up new situations and is interesting on account of the direction in which it is moving, Exploration.

(b) Activity which, generally speaking, moves within an established continuum and is interesting in respect of the use it makes of limited resources, Cultivation.

That is to say, some conduct calls attention to itself because of the magnitude of the displacements it brings about. But other conduct is interesting because of the relative absence of such displacements. And when this is so we are provoked to interpret it in terms of already revealed dispositions, in terms of 'character'.

For example, a composer may produce a piece of work which breaks entirely new ground; neither he, nor anyone else, has done anything like it before. On the other hand, he may produce a piece of work with nothing unexpected in it, nothing new except that it is another revelation of what we know him to be capable of. And when this is so we recognise it as, for example, 'a characteristic work of his middle period'. In short, 'character' appears when our attention is drawn to recurrences in conduct rather than genuine novelties.

Now, it is to be expected that the activity of governing and the experience of being governed may, in certain places and in certain periods of time, be interesting, not because it is changing rapidly and greatly, but because it seems to be displaying certain already revealed dispositions or character- istics. It seems to have settled into a kind of groove, and it is interesting on account of the use being made of a certain limited stock of ideas, images, beliefs, desires, projects, prac- tices, expedients and so on. Of course it is not to be expected that this activity will not at some future time reach out towards something new, that it will not add to its stock; but, for the moment, it seems to be exploiting what is already there rather than looking for something fresh. And 'what is already there' may be regarded as its current 'character'.

A 'character', then, is a groove or channel or rut into which, not only the conduct of individuals is apt from time to time to settle, but also such activities as commerce or politics. It happens when a trader is intent, not upon improving his product or finding new markets, but upon exploiting an already known market; it happens when a writer has, as we say, found a style for himself and is intent, not upon changing it, but using it; and it may be supposed to happen in the activity of governing. A 'character' is, of course, a rut or channel which has been excavated by human choices; and it establishes itself by long-continued movement which gradually chisels out its own restrictions, each absence of deviation contributing to a balance of dispositions which in the course of time discloses itself unmistakably. There is nothing magic or unusual about it: it is something that is always happening; and when it happens it may be made the subject of enquiry. An enquiry of this sort has taken place intermittently in relation to the politics of modern Europe, and I want now to consider the character of this enquiry and the assumptions upon which it has been conducted.

The hypothesis of this enquiry into the character of modern European politics is that it has a 'character' to be investigated; that is to say, that during a more or less definable period of time, political activity and the activity of governing reveals itself to have certain dispositions which are used, exploited, perhaps cultivated but which are not significantly added to, and that there is no marked propensity to seek others. The hypothesis does not, of course, exclude secular movement from the politics concerned, but it supposes it to be relatively insignificant.

Now, the proposition that the politics and government of a particular European state during a short period may reveal a 'character' of this sort is commonplace. British government in the mid-eighteenth century discloses an unmistakable 'character', and so also does the *ancien regime* in France. And it may be instructive to enquire into these characters. But the hypothesis we are considering is much more extensive: it supposes that the politics and government of Western European communities in post-medieval times (that is to say, at least from the mid-sixteenth century to our own day) reveals a 'character' of this sort sufficiently well-marked to make the study of it profitable. And in seeking to test the worth of this hypothesis what has to be shown is first, that somewhere about the beginning of this period, as a result of secular changes, significantly new political conditions had come to establish themselves, conditions likely to provoke new political aspirations, beliefs, projects and practices; and secondly that these have since remained relatively unchanged. Without the appearance of new political conditions of this sort there would be nothing to distinguish the politics of modern Europe from that of the Middle Ages; and unless these conditions were established and remained relatively unaltered there would be little opportunity for fixed political dispositions to make their appearance.

Now, it is my belief that during the sixteenth century, as a result of a long process in which the conditions of medieval politics and government were gradually modified, a new political condition had begun to establish itself; and further, that this condition has since remained unchanged except that each of its characteristics have established themselves more firmly.

Stated briefly, this condition displays four important characteristics.

(a) The activity of governing recognized as a 'sovereign' activity.

(b) Governments enjoying power so far in excess of anything that the earlier history of European politics has to show, that it gave a new quality to government.

(c) Subjects disposed to make choices for themselves about what they shall do and what they shall believe.

(d) Subjects indisposed or unable to make choices for themselves in spite of large opportunities.

Let us consider each of these in turn.

(a) The recognition of governing as a 'sovereign' activity, that is, the recognition of a single governing authority which, in virtue of its composition, is acknowledged to be supreme over all other authorities, proof against prescription, subject to no appeal and without external superior or partner – this understanding of the activity of governing emerged slowly over the European political horizon during the sixteenth century, and has remained with us ever since. The constitutional struggles of modern European history have all been concerned with who shall wield an authority of this sort; none of the participants in these struggles was ever in doubt that this was the question to be decided. And insofar as modern European political reflection has addressed itself to the question: what is the proper constitution for a government?, it has always been assumed that what was being discussed was the proper constitution of a 'sovereign' government.

Now, this was a very great change from what had hitherto been thought about government. In the Middle Ages governments were not 'sovereign' in this sense and it was never thought proper that they should be. In the first place, two authorities were recognized in a medieval society – the *regnum* and the *sacerdotium*. Secondly, the supremacy in the secular field which came to be enjoyed by the king fell far short of 'sovereignty', and even where representative assemblies were partners in government the composite authority of king and parliament was not thought of as wielding sovereign authority. And thirdly, no medieval government was ever recognised to be proof against prescription. There were known processes by which current rights might be redistributed, by which the law might be emended or added to, but there was no known authority by means of which a community could take complete command over its public arrangements, its law, customs and institutions, to do with them exactly what it thought fit.

The process in which the understanding of governing as a sovereign authority emerged and established itself was a long and intricate modification of medieval ideas and practices of government. I can say nothing about it here except to notice that it entailed the abolition of the independent authority of the *sacerdotium*, and that it was not complete until the authority of statute was recognized to be elsewhere absolute even over natural law. And to notice also that on its emergence sovereign government took a variety of forms: that is to say, the composition which a government should have in order to qualify for sovereignty found no uniform answer.

(b) A sovereign government is not necessarily a very powerful government. Certainly it is apt, other things being equal, to be more powerful than a government not recognized to be sovereign: it disposes of the power which comes from the absence of any legitimate competing authority. But a monopoly, although it is without partner or competitor, need not be remarkable for the power it exercises or for the displacements it is able to bring about. For a government to enjoy sole and absolute authority to make, emend, repeal and administer the laws of an association is one thing; for it to command enough power to control (for example) all the comings and goings, the pursuits and activities, of its subjects, is another thing. Nevertheless, it is a feature of all modern governments that they enjoy immense resources of power; even the least powerful of them is more powerful than any government of earlier times.

By 'having power' I mean, in this connection, having control over, or having the ability to control, the world of men and of things. It is being able (in respect of things) to act quickly, economically, certainly, with the desired effect and as little hindered as may be by the undesired consequences of action; and in respect of men it is the ability to formulate purposes clearly, to make them known in utterances that readily reach and are understood by those who are involved either as agents or as subjects, to enlist continuous support or to compel continuous acquiescence by decisive command, by provoking with certainty appropriate habits of conduct and by the imposition of economical and inescapable sanctions.

The power that has been acquired by or has fallen to modern governments derives from many sources, the chief of which is the share that governments have appropriated for themselves from the generally enhanced ability to control the behaviour of things and the conduct of men which is a feature of modern European civilization. This ability to control has, of course, increased immensely during the last four centuries, but nearly all of the means now at the disposal of governments were beginning to be available and to be used in the sixteenth century: the apparatus of enquiries, records, registers, files, dossiers, indexes, passports, identity cards and licences; ready and accurate information about the activities and dispositions of the subjects and the natural resources of a territory; maps and more accurate means of measuring time; ease of movement and communication; effective means of personal identification by names, signatures, fingerprints and photographs; efficient techniques of finance and accounting; settled and guarded frontiers; military and police forces easily mobilized and supplied with uniform equipment and powerful weapons. These and a thousand other adjuncts of power have come to distinguish the governments of modern times from any that went before, to determine their activities and enterprises.

(c and d) The third new feature of the modern European political scene is the character of the subjects of governments. I have already said something about this and need say little more now. These subjects are distinguished on account of their emancipation from the communal ties, occupations and communal organizations which characterized medieval society. But this emancipation generated two types of subject. On the one hand there were those who took the path of individuality, who created and extended opportunities for engaging in self-chosen activities and entertaining self-chosen beliefs and opinions. And in respect of these a modern society tended to an association of individuals choosing for themselves what they shall do and what they shall believe, engaging in a vast variety of rapidly changing and often competing activities, entertaining a vast variety of rapidly changing opinions, identifying their happiness with making these choices for themselves, and, in the course of time, generating a morality appropriate to their character. These subjects knew what they wanted from government: they wanted to be assured of the necessary conditions for the conduct of their enterprises, they wanted arrangements which released them from the collisions with one another which were apt to occur, and they wanted, not privileges for themselves, but their interests turned into rights which all should be eligible to enjoy. And these wants required for their satisfaction a 'sovereign' government. On the other hand, the desuetude of communal ties threw up, also, subjects unable or indisposed to make choices for themselves, subjects waiting to be told what to do and what to believe, and looking to their governments for care, protection and leadership. And these wants required for their satisfaction governments not only sovereign but also powerful.

It would appear, then, that conditions were emerging in the sixteenth century capable of provoking a mere political 'character' – conditions of politics and government significantly different from what had gone before. It is my belief that the subsequent history of political activity and reflection has been, very largely, a history in which this new political character was cultivated, in which its possibilities were explored and in which its limits were not significantly over-stepped. But whether or not this is so, what had emerged was something capable of investigation: the task of reflection was to ascertain exactly what had happened, and to study and interpret the activity of governing and the experience of being governed in these new circumstances. And the question to be decided was: what method shall be used in fulfilling this task?

Various methods were proposed and pursued; and interpretation went on at a variety of levels. The problems which appeared at the philosophical level engaged the attention of writers such as Hobbes, Locke, Hume, Rousseau, Kant, Hegel, Mill and others; and we shall have to consider later what they had to say. Other writers, partisan in their approach, explored the possibilities of this new character from the point of view of one or other of the two classes of subjects which composed

35

these new associations. But there were some writers who set themselves the task of simply ascertaining the dispositions of this new political 'character', and most notable among these was Montesquieu. The method he chose was one in which ideal models were made of the dispositions of this character, and the possibilities of the character explored in this manner.

Writing in the mid-eighteenth century, Montesquieu was handicapped in his observation by the fact that the 'character' of modern politics was as yet only imperfectly revealed. For, although its main features may be said to have been visible as early as the middle of the sixteenth century, it took a considerable time before it established itself unmistakably. What is remarkable about Montesquieu is that he was able to perceive as much as he did: his most notable characteristic is his sensibility for what was afoot but as yet only half-revealed.

The project of *De L'Esprit des Lois* is nothing less than to ascertain and to interpret the new character which was being acquired by modern European politics and government. Montesquieu's *Esprit* is, in fact, what I have called 'character'. His enterprise is to investigate, not laws and government in general, but the current dispositions in respect of government. Of course there is much else in his large and miscellaneous book; he explores a great variety of questions in an often disorderly manner, and he is often remembered most for some of his peripheral observations – the relation of climate to government, for example, and the so-called principle of the separation of powers of government – but his central theme is the possibilities contained in the political character which Europe had come to acquire.

Neglecting some of the refinements and rearranging a little the rather disordered observations contained in *De L'Esprit des Lois*, Montesquieu can be understood to be saying that there are three possible species of government. These are, of course, ideal models, and it is irrelevant to suggest that they have nowhere existed exactly as he describes them. Like Aristotle, whom he follows clearly, he is concerned to investigate, not actual regimes, but ideal types which, as we shall see later, he takes to represent the possibilities of the modern European political character.

He denotes these three species of government as

(a) Despotism.

(b) Monarchy and aristocratic republicanism.

(c) Democracy.

At first sight it would appear that he understands them as types of government specified by their constitutions, and in particular by the number of persons who participate in the activity of governing. And, indeed, Book II of the *Esprit des Lois* is devoted to a consideration of the structure of each sort of government. But it soon becomes clear that what he is really interested in is not the composition of governments, but their activities and the appropriateness of these activities to the character of their subjects; not how these governments are constituted, but what they are disposed to do and the effect of this upon the character of their subjects. Each of these expressions stands for a specific manner of governing. And the task Montesquieu has set himself is to investigate how each of these manners of governing discloses itself in a characteristic attitude towards law and the administration of justice, towards liberty, towards the dispositions and conditions of life of its subjects, and towards their political education. In short, he illustrates the contention that the main interest of modern European political reflection is in the activities and not the constitutions of governments, and that this main interest is often obscured because most of the expressions in our political vocabulary refer (in the first place) to constitutions and, instead of inventing new expressions, we have converted them to new uses. Despotism, monarchy and democracy, then, stand for governments active in specific manners and not for governments composed in certain manners.

DESPOTISM

The principle of despotism is fear. The despot governs his subjects in his own interests, and the activity of governing is an activity of exploitation. Except where rules may be convenient to the despot (which will not be very often) there will be no laws, and consequently no courts of law. All offences will be offences against the despot himself or his agents, and will be punished with the greatest severity. The condition of the subjects of a despot is one of servitude and equality: all are equally slaves and all, in the end, are equally insecure. The activities of subjects will be unenterprising because their fruits and their duration will always be uncertain. Nevertheless, there will be a certain straining after the enjoyment of luxury whenever the possibility of it occurs: 'a slave appointed by his master to tyrannize over his other slaves, uncertain of enjoying tomorrow the blessings of today, has no other happiness but that of gratifying the arrogance, the passions and the enjoyments of the moment'. In short, the engagements and activities of subjects will be marked by the indolence and the excess which belongs to whatever is shortlived. Since subjects will fear one another as much as they fear the despot himself, there will be little room for friendship or trustful social intercourse. And the object of political education will be to inculcate servility and blind obedience to the commands of the despot, and it will consequently entail a systematic debasement of the mind.

MONARCHY AND ARISTOCRATIC REPUBLICANISM

I put these two species of government together because, although Montesquieu distinguishes between them, the distinction he observes is almost entirely in respect of the different manners in which they are constituted: there is very little if any distinction between them in respect of the manner in which they are disposed to be active. In other words, they are united in a single understanding of the office of government. And this goes to show that Montesquieu did not make the mistake (so common in his time) of supposing that the manner in which a government is composed and authorized determines the manner in which it governs.

The principle of this species of government – which I will call 'monarchy' for short – is honour. By 'honour' Montesquieu means an aristocratic virtue but one which need not be confined to an aristocracy. He means the natural pride and dignity of a man who feels himself to be an individual among individuals, to be responsible for his own conduct, and who, because he is self-confident in making his own choices, is able to be frank without being arrogant. The ideal type of the character Montesquieu has in mind is, I think, the *megalopsychos* of Aristotle, the magnanimous man; but, of course, he did not expect everyone in whom this disposition was uppermost to conform exactly to the ideal type. As Montesquieu describes him, the man of honour is a man whose virtue is not understood as conduct which he owes to others or to his society so much as to himself: he is a self-contained man who recognizes

mean and ignoble conduct as undignified, a relapse into bar-
barism, a denigration of himself.

Monarchy, then, is government appropriate to such subjects,
and is government in the interests of such subjects. To govern,
here, is neither to exploit nor to lead, but simply to rule. The
laws of an association of such subjects (who may be said
almost to exult in their individuality) are few and precise, and
they are administered in independent courts whose judges are
not amenable to extraneous pressures. Offences are, in the
main, offences not against the ruler, nor against the society
itself (which is understood to be an association of individuals),
but against 'others' or 'another'. The condition of the subjects
of 'monarchy' is one of freedom and of equality – an equality
which is uninsistent because it is an equality of status and not
of condition. The activities of these subjects are many and
various because they spring from the exercise of individual
choice; and, for the same reason, they are not concerned merely
with the common necessities of life. But (on account of the
confidence with which they are engaged) they easily avoid
that excessive straining after luxury characteristic of the subjects of a despot. Social intercourse is free, unhindered by fear
of the ruler, and uninhibited by feelings of superiority or
inferiority. And the object of political education is to inculcate
these virtues of honour and moderation; in other words, to fit a
man for membership of such an association of self-determined
individuals.

DEMOCRACY

The principle of this species of government is virtue, by which
Montesquieu means care for the public or common good. Here,
then, there is recognized to be, not an association, but a
genuine community; and governing is in the interests of this
community. It is not an activity of exploitation, nor is it an
activity merely of ruling; it is an activity of leadership, the
management of the affairs of a concern. The office of government is to interpret authoritatively the common good of the
community and to impose it upon all its members.

In this manner of governing there will be laws, indeed there
will be comprehensive laws, in which, for the most part,
sin and crime will not be distinguished. All the laws will be
summed up in a single commandment: act so as to promote the

common good. Here *salus populi* is recognized to be the supreme law informing all laws, and where necessary overriding the administration of particular laws. These laws will be administered in courts, which will tend to have the character of 'peoples' courts' whose care is, not so much to see that the letter of the laws is observed but to see that the common good is on no occasion prejudiced. Where, in such a community, virtue is widespread, punishments need not be severe; and there will be a disposition to believe that prevention is better than punishment. All offences will be recognized as offences against the community; private law relationships will be small in number and insignificant. The subjects of this government will enjoy equality: each is equally a servant of the community and has a right to an equal share in the products of communal activity. They will enjoy security rather than liberty; security being recognized as a reward for serving the community. The activities of these subjects will not spring from individual choice, but from a common desire to serve the common good as interpreted by the government. These activities will be directed towards the provision of the necessities of life for all equally: luxury will be frowned upon as an undue share in the common product, and frugality will be counted a virtue. Individuality, or any suspicion of superiority in taste or enterprise, will arouse resentment, and a common mediocrity of ability and fortune will be recognized as appropriate in such a community. And the object of political education will be to inculcate, not merely subservience to the common good, but the love of it; not merely acquiescent conduct, but behaviour which has the love of the Republic as its motive.

How to construe all this as an account of merely possible forms of government mainly from the point of view, not of their constitutions but of their pursuits and their relations to their subjects, would be to understand the *Esprit des Lois* as no more than an academic exercise. What, I think, Montesquieu is giving us is something much more significant: it is an analysis of the dispositions of a current political character. In the manner of a medieval allegorist – the author of the *Romance of the Rose*, for example – who personifies the dispositions of a single character and makes each speak in utterances appropriate to the mood it represents, Montesquieu discloses in three simple and ideal types of government what he believes to be the dispositions of a single complex political character, dispositions each of which is a potentiality which may or may not be realized in fact. And what we have to enquire into is, first, the cogency of the analysis; and secondly, the significance of the conclusions Montesquieu draws from it.

The suggestion we have before us is that the modern European character is not *capable de tout*, but capable of a certain range of dispositions in respect of the pursuits and engagements of government. And the significant points in this range of dispositions are despotism, monarchy and democracy. This does not mean that the regimes of modern Europe will necessarily be close approximations to one of these three; it means that in each of the actual regimes there will be found tendencies which, if pushed, may result in one or other of these regimes. Despotism, monarchy and democracy are, so to speak, the aptitudes of the modern European political character. And Montesquieu makes his view of things more plausible by recognizing that some of these aptitudes are, in fact, stronger than others. The weakest of them is despotism; indeed it is so weak that it may almost be said to fall outside the capabilities of the modern European political character. It is a species of government, in Montesquieu's understanding, unlikely to appear in a temperate climate; and further, the servility of character required in the subjects of a despot is remote from the sort of people who have come to inhabit Western Europe. With this qualification, I think it is fair to conclude that Montesquieu's analysis of the modern European political character is acute; indeed, remarkably acute when one considers how imperfectly this character had revealed itself in his day.

But to what purpose does Montesquieu propose to put this analysis? What conclusions does he think may be drawn from it? There are, I think, two conclusions, and both of them disclose unmistakably the Aristotelian frame of Montesquieu's thought.

(a) First, he believes that, with the exception of despotism, which is corrupt by nature, each of these regimes is capable of being good of its kind. Each is subject to characteristic corruptions: monarchy has a tendency to degenerate into despotism, and democracy has a tendency to degenerate into the sort of monarchy which springs from a distrust of the constituted rulers and the desire of every man to have a finger in government. Despotism occurs whenever a regime deserts its proper principle: when monarchy deserts the principle of honour, and when in a democracy equality becomes either extinct or extreme. But, in certain circumstances, each may be recognized as a viable and an appropriate regime. And the most important circumstances to be taken account of in this connection are, in his opinion, the geographical situation and the size of the society, its past history, and the religion and principal occupations of the subjects.

(b) But Montesquieu wishes to draw a second sort of conclusion. He thinks his analysis is capable of yielding a decision about the best sort of government. That is, he believes that one of these dispositions of the modern European political character is better and more appropriate than the others. The principle on which this decision is reached is the Aristotelian principle that the best is a mean between extremes. And in Montesquieu's view, what he calls monarchy is a mean between the extremes of despotism and democracy: each is an excess to be avoided, and each is an excess which is avoided in what he calls monarchy. And perhaps it is worth noting that Montesquieu had more than a suspicion that despotism and democracy have something in common: that democracy has a propensity to become a sort of despotism. But the events which might be considered to provide some sort of verification of this hypothesis lay still in the future.

In the end, I suppose, Montesquieu's answer to the question: why do you think what you call monarchy is a better manner of governing than either despotism or democracy? would not have been the merely formal answer; because monarchy is a mean between extremes. His manner of thinking encourages us to believe that he would point to the current conditions of European life, and in particular to the acquired character of the subjects of European governments, and would conclude that monarchy is better because it is the manner of governing appropriate to these conditions and to the character of these subjects.

And here, I think, he would show himself to be taking too restricted a view. If what I have suggested is true, if the subjects of modern governments do not show a single disposition but two obliquely opposed dispositions – that of the 'individual' and that of the 'anti-individual' – then it would seem that Montesquieu's 'monarchy' and 'democracy' are manners of governing which reflect respectively the observed propensities of modern European character; 'monarchy' being the manner of governing appropriate to 'individuality' and democracy to 'anti-individuality'. And consequently, we should expect the manner of governing in modern Europe to range between these two extremes, settling upon one or other of them only when and where one of these dispositions had, for the time being, decisively got the better of the other. But this again was more than we can expect Montesquieu to have seen: the 'anti-individualist' disposition had not, in his time, revealed itself unmistakably.

But whatever we may think about Montesquieu's own conclusions, about the character of modern European politics, the *Esprit des Lois* represents a manner of thinking about politics and government which has been unduly neglected, which has not yet yielded all it is capable of yielding and which it is still profitable to pursue.

PART II

THE POLITICAL THEORY
OF INDIVIDUALISM

4

LOCKE: THE THEOLOGICAL VISION

We have noticed two aspects of the context of modern European political reflection: the conditions of government and the character of subjects on the one side, and the moral dispositions current in modern Europe on the other. Considered in this context, political reflection seems to disperse itself in two different directions, each of which corresponds to one of the two main classes of subjects which emerged in modern Europe and one of the two predominant moral dispositions. And both of these directions of thought are, for the reasons I have given, mainly concerned with an understanding of the office of government and only in a minor degree with the constitution of government. This is how I propose to arrange the material at our disposal. It gives a pattern to the history of political reflection which, like all patterns, is an interpretation. Other patterns can be imagined, and some others may be superior to the one I have chosen; but I have thought it better to give some pattern to this history, even if it is an artificial pattern, rather than none at all. And I think one of the main interests of the pattern I have chosen is that on occasion it makes up the conventional grouping of writers and establishes new lines of communication: Burke and Paine, for example, will be found joined with one another rather than opposed to one another; J.S. Mill sides with Comte rather than with Bentham.

I intend to consider first what I call the politics of individualism: and, as you will observe, this title reflects one of the two major moral dispositions of modern Europe and one of the two major classes in European society.

By the politics of individualism I mean a certain understanding of the office of government which appeared slowly in response to the new conditions of government and which coincided with a moral disposition which also emerged gradually. The main outline of this understanding of the office of government is clear enough to us, who have had the advantage of four centuries of reflection on it; but to those who formulated it, especially the earlier writers, it was, of course, anything but clear. They were feeling their way in an intellectual enquiry designed to construe in terms of appropriate general principles one of the elements in a current manner of governing and a moral feeling which was gradually establishing itself as a coherent disposition.

The situation to which the activity of governing has to be related is understood to be something like this. I and my neighbours, my associates, my friends and my compatriots, are people engaged in a great variety of activities. We are apt to entertain a multiplicity of opinions on every conceivable subject and are disposed to change these beliefs as we grow tired of them or as they prove unserviceable. Each of us is pursuing a course of his own; and there is no project so unlikely that somebody will not be found to engage in it, no enterprise so foolish that somebody will not undertake it. We are all inclined to be passionate about our own concerns, whether it is making things or selling them, whether it is business or sport, religion or learning. Each of us has preferences of his own and we connect happiness with being able to indulge these preferences. Some dream dreams of new and better worlds, others are more inclined to move in familiar paths or even to be idle. We enter into relationships of interest, of emotion, of competition, partnership, guardianship, love, friendship, jealousy and hatred, some of which are more durable than others. We make agreements with one another, we have expectations about one another's conduct; we approve, we are indifferent and we disapprove.

This multiplicity of activity and variety of opinion is apt to produce collisions: we pursue courses which cut across those of others, and we do not all approve of the same sort of conduct. But, in the main, we get along with one another, sometimes by giving way, sometimes by standing fast, sometimes in a compromise. Our conduct consists of activity assimilated to that of others in numberless small, and for the most part unconsidered, adjustments.

THE POLITICAL THEORY OF INDIVIDUALISM

Now, in what I have called the politics of individualism this situation is accepted as the current condition of human circumstances. As we shall see, when reflection gets to work theories explaining why and how this situation emerged are expounded. Attempts are made to show it as a good, or even as the best possible, situation; it will be contended that it represents unalterable 'human nature', or a divine dispensation or an unfortunate lapse from the designs of God. But, for the moment, all we need notice is the belief that this situation is the current situation of ourselves. And the question asked is: what in these circumstances is the proper office of government? And, again in brief outline, the answer given is something like this.

The office of government is not to impose other beliefs and activities upon its subjects, not to tutor or to educate them, not to make them better or happier in a way other than that which they have chosen for themselves, not to direct them, lead them or manage them; the office of government is merely to rule. And ruling is recognized as a specific and limited activity. The image of the ruler is not that of the manager but that of the umpire whose business it is to administer the rules of a game in which he does not himself participate.

Government, then, is not understood to begin with a vision of another, different and better, world, but with the observation of the self-government practised even by men of passion in the conduct of their enterprises; it begins in the informal adjustment of interests to one another which are designed to release those who are apt to collide from the mutual frustration of a collision. Sometimes these adjustments are no more than agreements between two parties to keep out of each other's way; sometimes they are of wider application and more durable character, such as the international rules for the prevention of collisions at sea.

This is where government begins. But the self-government of men of passionate belief and enterprise is apt to break down when it is most needed. It often suffices to resolve minor collisions of interest, but beyond these it is not to be relied upon. A more precise, a more authoritative and a less easily corrupted ritual is required to resolve the massive collisions which this manner of living is apt to generate and to release the participants from the massive frustrations in which they are apt to become locked. The custodian of this ritual is 'the government', and the rules it imposes are 'the law'.

49

To govern, then, is to provide a *vinculum juris* for those manners of conduct which, in the circumstances, are least likely to result in a frustrating collision of interests; to provide redress and compensation for those who suffer from others behaving in a contrary manner; sometimes to provide punishment for those who pursue their own interests regardless of the rules; and, of course, to provide a sufficient force to maintain the authority of an arbiter of this kind, and to protect the association from the degredation of its enemies. And since the current condition of human circumstance is one in which new activities are constantly appearing and rapidly extending themselves, and in which beliefs and opinions are perpetually being modified or discarded in favour of others – that is, a condition of incessant and rapid change – the office of government is to be alert to recognize emergent occasions of collision and to modify the rules appropriately. For the rules to be inappropriate to current activities is as unprofitable as for them to be unfamiliar to those who have to obey them. In short, the office of government is to maintain a condition of stable equilibrium, a condition which makes profitable, even possible, the activities of subjects and their associates. The ruler is a stabilizer; governing is a placatory activity, an activity of reconciliation, in which failure is to be identified with a system of living that is either so loose that no subject has any reliable expectations about the activity of his neighbours, or so tight as to exclude or hinder the changes of activity and belief which, in these circumstances, are constantly pressing for recognition.

Now, long before this understanding of the office of government came to be construed by theorists in the idiom of general ideas, it appeared in a disposition to demand from rulers a style of governing something like this, and a disposition to endow governments with the characteristics necessary for governing in this style.

The seminal change was the emergence of subjects who had begun to taste the experience of individuality, of self-determination, and were eager to pursue it. This cannot be regarded as the simple cause of the modifications which were taking place in the practices of governments, but it was an overwhelmingly important condition of them. Aspiration, the aspiration to enjoy the experience of individuality, worked upon the materials of government, and each modified the other.

Stated negatively, the demands of those subjects were for an instrument of government, itself purged of the relics of feudal privilege, and one at once able and disposed to put an end to feudal ties and feudal immunities wherever they had survived. But to abrogate feudal privilege was not merely to annul certain current rights and restrictions; it was to abrogate a situation in which persons, on account of their exclusive status, enjoyed immunity from duties which were the common lot of the rest of their compatriots. And what was demanded, and what in fact flowed in to fill the vacancy, was not a condition in which a new and similarly exclusive class enjoyed newly acquired immunities, but one in which all subjects alike were to enjoy the same rights and to suffer the same duties. In other words, the demand of those who enjoyed the experience of individuality was for the rights and duties appropriate for this enjoyment to be established, not for themselves as a privilege, but for all subjects without exception.

In positive terms, the demand of current individuality was for a manner of government capable of transforming the interests of individuality into a system of rights common to all subjects. This demand gradually crystallized into a demand for a determined, centralized, sovereign government. Determination was required in order to emancipate government itself from the relics of feudal privilege; a single centralized governing authority was recognized (in the sixteenth century as in the French Revolution) as the means by which the subject might be emancipated from conduct shaped and determined by innumerable, half-concealed and wholly uncontrolled communal pressures; government recognized as a sovereign activity, that is to say, as an activity not bound by prescription, was the only means by which the emergent interests of individuality might be transformed into rights. And in response to these demands, governments of this sort appeared. They were not all of them of the same construction: so-called 'absolute' monarchies emerged side by side with incipient parliamentary governments. But they were all disposed and equipped to comply with these demands; and in their hands legislative activity, recognized as a sovereign activity, first appeared in modern Europe.

Sovereign governments, then, were called for and they made their appearance. But did the aspirations of individuality require also very powerful governments? This may be doubted. Governments with enough power to destroy current privileges were certainly required; but beyond this, those intent upon the enjoyment of individuality had an appropriate suspicion of the immense power which was coming to be acquired by modern European governments; and, as we shall see, it is a notable part of the theory of this style of governing, when it came to be constructed, to view exceedingly powerful government with suspicion, and to require that the authority of government should operate in a process of making law, and that the administration of this law should be in the hands of an independent judiciary. The so-called 'rule of law' was not, and was not regarded as, a specific safeguard of the interests of individuality; it was recognized as an emblem of the necessary conditions for the enjoyment of individuality.

This, then, was the general view of the office of government considered to be appropriate to subjects who had embarked upon the experience of individuality, and this was the sort of government which this experience promoted and gradually brought into being.

It was not long before the theorists set to work to elicit the general principles of this style of governing. They were preceded by observers who did little more than perceive and report what was afoot, and we have to wait until the seventeenth century for writers who engage themselves to theorize this political experience. Their reflections fell naturally into two parts: first, an attempt to *deduce* the individual who had already appeared as an empirical fact and to transform what was no more than a compelling impulse into a moral disposition; and secondly, an attempt to *deduce* the office of government appropriate to this individual, an office which also had already appeared as an empirical fact. And the differences between these writers are mainly concerned with different manners of accomplishing these two purposes.

You will expect me to spend most of my time considering the later writers, the writers of the eighteenth and nineteenth centuries, who took part in this intellectual enterprise. But you must allow me to dwell for a moment upon the writers who, in the seventeenth century, first began to explore this manner of thinking; for, as it happens, they were not only the first to do so in the modern world, but they also saw the problems to be tackled more clearly than many of their successors. The writings of these first theorists of the modern state are, of course, encumbered with relics from the past, and many of the idioms of their thought were later put on one side as unsatisfactory – or at least they became outmoded manners of thinking; but they were thinkers of great power and imagination who at least saw to the bottom of the task of anyone who wants to construct a political theory of individualism. The greatest of these were Spinoza, Thomas Hobbes and John Locke.

I propose to say nothing about Spinoza and Hobbes, though each in his own way constructed an almost perfectly integrated political theory in the individualist idiom. But it is worth while spending a little while on John Locke, because the very looseness of his thought, as well as its comparative simplicity, affords an excellent illustration of the problems to be faced by a political theory in this idiom.

It must be confessed that Locke is often a confused thinker, inadvertently qualifying his thoughts by others which carry him in quite a different direction. An attempt has been made to represent him as an early theorist in the collectivist idiom, but I do not think it can be sustained; it is plausible only when certain of his expressions are given an exaggerated interpretation. But, be that how it may, what I want to put before you now is, not so much an interpretation of Locke, as an account of his contribution to the political theory of individualism. Like other writers on politics, he has something to say about the proper constitution of a governing authority, but what we are concerned with here are his thoughts on the office of government: what a government should be doing.

What sort of a creature is a human being? He is a creature capable of two main activities: sense experience and introspection. All his thoughts, his judgements, his motives and his actions spring from the exercise of one or both of these capabilities. He has no 'innate' ideas, that is to say ideas with which he is born and which he has in common with any other creature of the same kind. What he has in common with his fellows is merely these capabilities. This means that each man is wholly responsible for his own experience; each makes his own choices and conducts his own life on the basis of judgements he makes by reflecting upon his own experience of the world. Things are good and evil to him only in relation to pleasure and pain – that is, in relation to his own sense experience. In short, he is, unavoidably, a self-determined individual. And this individualism has its roots, in Locke's theory, in a theory of knowledge.

Nevertheless, the experience of human beings may be said to acquaint them with a certain undeniable piece of information about themselves. It tells them that they are each 'the workmanship of one omnipotent and infinitely wise Maker, all are servants of one Sovereign Master, sent into the world by His order and about His business, they are His property'. The business of each man is, consequently, to carry out the will of his Maker, and this will is spoken of by Locke as the Law of God for mankind, or the Law of Nature. Knowledge of this law is not innate in human beings: it is gathered, like all other knowledge, from human experience of the world.

Now, from this, two undeniable conclusions may be drawn:

(a) Each human being is an independent servant of God's will, enjoying perfect freedom in respect of other human beings to choose and order his own conduct so long as it conforms to the Law of God. In other words, no man has any authority whatsoever over any other man: in respect of being servants of God all men are equal. Every man is absolute lord of his own person.

(b) It is the duty of each man to recognize every other man as his equal and to do nothing to harm him, frustrate him or hinder him as a servant of God.

Now, the human race, composed of these free, independent, self-determined, equal individuals has been set down in the world; and they are at liberty to make what impact they choose to make upon the world. The general condition of human life is that well-being is impossible without work – that is without *doing* something with the natural resources of the world, and when a man works he appropriates for his own use some part of the resources of the world. This, as Locke puts it, is acquiring property; and consequently every man may be said to have a God-given right to acquire property. And it would be a breach of the Law of God for one man to invade what another man, in carrying out the will of God, has appropriated for himself.

Nevertheless, the Law of God being a normative law, it is possible for human beings to disobey it. And, indeed, human experience tells us that they are apt to disobey it. Disobedience consists in frustrating another human being in the enjoyment of his rights under the Law of God. When this happens, however, the man who is frustrated must 'shift for himself', must assert his own rights, because, on earth, there is nobody else to whom he can appeal for protection. In other words, the administration of the Law of God is in the hands of each individual, who has the right and the duty to protect himself and his property.

This situation is described by Locke as one in which few and equal individuals are living in proximity to one another, enjoying and exploiting the resources of the natural world, without any common superior on earth, but with a duty to recognize the freedom and the equality of each other. Where this duty is breached, the man who suffers has the right to do everything in his power to reassert the Law of God on his own behalf.

This is, clearly, a not altogether satisfactory situation. It would be improved if:

(a) Each man did not have to depend upon his own experience for a knowledge of the Law of God; that is, if there were some authoritative statement of this law, recognized by all men.

(b) Each man, when a dispute arose, could appeal to an independent umpire; that is, if each man were not under the necessity, when he thought he was suffering from an invasion of his rights as a servant of God, of being judge in his own cause and the executor of his own judgement.

In short, what would make things easier and more orderly would be an umpire who had authority to act at two levels – the two levels at which human beings are apt to collide with one another:

(a) An umpire to judge and to decide between the various current interpretations of what are and what are not the duties of each man under the Law of God.

(b) An umpire to judge and to decide disputes, not about the contents of the Law of God, but about the operation of the law in particular situations, and with power to enforce his decisions.

In other words, it would clearly be more convenient if each individual were not left to shift for himself, but if all individuals who lived in proximity to one another came to recognize an umpire of this sort as a common superior. And to live in a condition in which an umpire of this sort is recognized is to live under what Locke calls a 'government', to live in a civil society.

The activity of governing is, then, as Locke understands it, an activity of 'umpirage'. It is an activity which requires 'authority', and it introduces into the situation an element of 'subordination' – all are equally 'subordinate' to the authority of the umpire, and his decision is final.

The ruler as 'umpire' is not a leader, or a manager of the lives and activities of his subjects. Government understood in this manner assumes that subjects will continue to make their own choices for themselves, to enjoy and to cultivate their individuality, to be responsible for their own salvation; the only 'sovereign' they know is their 'sovereign Maker', God himself. Locke does not attribute sovereignty to government; only the office of umpirage. And it is an office that comes into play only where a collision between two or more subjects has taken place.

And this recognition of the indestructable value of individuality is made all the more clear in what Locke says about the end or purpose of government. Its purpose is not to deprive a subject of his self-determination: it is to preserve his liberty and his property, to secure him in his enjoyment of his property, to provide a 'sanctuary' into which he may retire if his rights as a servant of God are infringed. The ruler does not provide his subjects with rights and duties; these they already have from the Law of God and they need no others. What the ruler provides is a means of redress to any subject who is denied, by the action of his neighbour, the enjoyment of his rights. In other words, what the ruler has to umpire is collisions between two or more of his subjects. And so far there can be no doubt about Locke's enterprise: it is to construct a version of the political theory of individualism.

But there is something more to be noticed: civil society does create something new – a new situation. There appears for the first time something that may be called 'a common or public good'. The good of each man remains what it always was, to play his part as a servant of God. But now, in addition to this, he and all his fellow subjects have a common good or a common interest in maintaining the authority of the umpire upon which rests their opportunity to enjoy their rights. There is a 'good of the community'. But here, again, a careful reading of Locke leaves us in no doubt that when he speaks of 'the good of the community' he is not diverging into a collectivist political theory: 'the good of the community' is nothing more or less than this narrow and specific good – the maintenance of the authority of the umpire or ruler. It is, properly speaking, not '*the* common good', but *a* good which all subjects have in common.

THE POLITICAL THEORY OF INDIVIDUALISM

So far, then, what we find in Locke is a version of an individualist political theory. He understands the activity of ruling and the office of government not as depriving the subject of his 'lordship over his own person', but as a means by which he may have the unhindered enjoyment of that lordship insofar as it is consistent with the Law of God.

And the individualist cast of Locke's thought becomes absolutely unmistakable when we enquire into his notion of the manner in which this umpire is enstated and authorized. No man may be legitimately subordinated to another, as a subject is to his ruler, except by his own *consent*.

There are, of course, all sorts of difficulties connected with this notion of consent; but what is quite clear in Locke is that he intends to indicate by it the indestructable self-determination of the individual human being. The authority of the umpire rests solely and only upon the consent of each of his subjects. And to re-enforce this, Locke imagines it to be the right of each child when he or she comes of age to choose what civil society he or she shall give allegiance to.

Indeed, in Locke's view the authorization of a ruler is a process in which each subject gives his individual consent in two stages. First, he consents to recognize the decisions of 'the majority' as his own decisions and to be bound by them; and secondly (in certain forms of government), he may recognize the authority of a set of people who are not themselves a majority but who are taken to 'represent' the majority. And this notion of the authority of the majority serves to re-emphasize Locke's individualist premises: there is no attempt to dissolve the individuality of each subject into anything like a 'general will'; only the choice and resolve of individual persons can authorize the subjection of one man to the authority of another.

And there is one more point to notice. The ruling authority, however it may be constituted, this umpire, is in the position of a *trustee*: to govern is to undertake a trust. And this coincides with a feature in the general account of the political theory of individualism that I have put before you. The individual is not afraid of the authority of an umpire. He knows that the umpire's decision must be final and he knows that the exercise of his individuality, his capability of making choices for himself, depends upon this finality. But he is unavoidably nervous of the umpire overstepping the terms of his office, apprehensive that the ruler may use the power which he must have as an umpire to engage in activities which do not properly belong to an umpire. The business of the umpire as legislator is to decide, when dispute arises, what is the contents of the Law of Nature or of God; the business of the umpire as judge is to resolve the collisions of those whose activities cut across one another; and consequently, it is highly important for the political theorist of individuality to show how the power of the umpire may be limited to that which is necessary for the performance of the duties of his office. In Locke's understanding of the situation, the umpire who oversteps his office commits a breach of 'trust'.

It would appear, then, that Locke's contribution to the political theory of individualism is a strange and characteristic mixture of philosophy and simple-mindedness. A foundation for his individualism may be found in his theory of knowledge: the structure and capabilities of the human mind are such that each man is a separate individual who can surrender that individuality, or any part of it, only by an action of his own, by his own choice. This is Locke's attempt to deduce philosophically the historically achieved individuality of the world in which he lived.

But beside this, Locke places a theological doctrine in which individuality is the character each man has of being an equal and independent servant of God. Individuality is the gift of an omnipotent and infinitely wise Maker. Things might have been different, men might have been made with a character other than this, but it so happens that this is their character. This, perhaps, is a less than philosophical generalization of the achieved individuality of Locke's world, but it is not for that reason to be neglected. Indeed, I believe that to Locke, the Puritan who became the father of European liberalism, this theological conception was more important than anything else. It is the responsibility that each man has for his own salvation which, in the end, determines his individuality.

5

KANT, ADAM SMITH AND BURKE

So far, I have put before you some general reflections on the political theory of individualism and shown you how it appears in the somewhat simple version of John Locke. This version may, perhaps, be said to fall short of being a properly philosophical version on account of its appeal to religious belief in its attempt to deduce individuality.

The view I am suggesting to you is that the starting-point of all this reflection is an historical achievement, the high level of individuality which emerged among Western European peoples as the counterpart of the desuetude of feudal societies. And the problem of political theory was to understand this phenomenon rationally, not merely empirically, and to disclose the sort of social order and government it entailed. And it is in tackling the first of these problems that Locke makes his retreat upon religious belief: his individual is revealed as the special creation of an omnipotent and all-wise God.

In studying the subsequent history of the political theory of individualism, we shall find that much of it is concerned with writers who, in one respect or another, fall short of a properly philosophical treatment of individuality. But, before going further, I want to put before you a treatment of this problem which, I think, comes nearer than any other to being properly philosophical, namely that of Immanuel Kant.

Kant: The Supremacy of Self-determination

Human beings, according to Kant's view of things, disclose two ineradicable dispositions: (a) A disposition to be self-determined; and (b) A disposition to associate with others of their kind.

(a) The disposition to be self-determined is a disposition for each man to decide things for himself, to make his own choices, to determine the directions in which his own happiness lies and to move in those directions; in short, a disposition to free himself from natural necessity and an ability to live according to his own choices, and not to have his movements determined on all occasions by the impact of the external world upon him. This disposition and capability is, in the first place, rational. Every time a man who receives a punch on the nose does not react like an automaton, but considers and chooses what he shall do in response, he is exercising his disposition to be a 'rational' being, to be self-determined, to be 'free' and not in bondage to natural necessity.

Further, without this disposition and capacity to be an individual, morality would be impossible: indeed, in Kant's view, individuality is both the product and the condition of the moral consciousness. In moral activity a man is being determined not by his natural inclinations, nor by the operation upon him of various pleasurable or painful stimuli, but by a choice which he makes for himself: he determines to do what he believes to be his *duty*. Morality is concerned with the realization of freedom by the resolute pursuit of rational, chosen ends in opposition to those of natural inclination. And consequently, the goodness of an action is related solely and only to the motive from which it is performed: if moral goodness consisted in doing actions which achieve certain results, if it consisted in the impact of a man's conduct upon the external world, then moral goodness would be at the mercy of chance and the natural order of the world, and the link between freedom and goodness would have been broken.

But, as Kant understands it, if a human being claims this right to be an individual, to be self-determined, it follows that each man must recognize a similar right in every other man. To deny the right of self-determination to others is to remove the foundation upon which a man claims it for himself, because he claims it for himself on account of his being a man, on account (that is) of the character he shares with every other man. Hence, the fundamental rule of the moral and rational human life is to cultivate one's own individuality and recognize the right of all other men to cultivate their own individualities; or, as Kant says, to treat all other men as you claim to be treated yourself – as an end, and not as a means to somebody else's end. And further, it follows that no man has the right to impose his own moral judgments upon any other man: it is, says Kant,

> a contradiction to regard myself as in duty bound to promote the perfection of another; for it is just in this that the perfection of another man as a person consists, namely, that he is able *of himself* to set before himself his own end according to his own notion of duty; and it is a contradiction to make it a duty for me to do something which no other but he himself can do.

Here, then, is Kant's theory of the disposition to be an individual. He connects it with rationality and morality. But if he were asked, how does it come about that human beings have this capacity for self-determination, and why should it be cultivated rather than suppressed?, I suppose his answer would be not unlike Locke's answer. He would say, this is the character of a human being, this is what distinguishes him from an animal, this is how God made him. And he is only more philosophical than Locke on account of taking longer to get back to this fundamental belief: the mediation between the empirical observation of human behaviour and the rational idea of human character is more subtle and more elaborate.

(b) The second disposition of human character – the disposition to associate with others – Kant rationalizes in terms of utility and, in the end, in terms of self-preservation. But the supremely important thing is to understand that even where this disposition to associate is cultivated, and men find a manner of associating with one another, the primary disposition to be an individual, to be self-determined and to make one's own choices for oneself, remains. And not only does it remain; it is also identified as the source of all human progress. Everything of value in a civilized manner of living is the product of the exercise and cultivation of individuality, is the product of the competitive propensities of mankind. A civil society is never more than an association of individuals.

Man, then, as a rational and moral being, is capable of self-determination: he has internal freedom, and nothing that can happen to him can deprive him of this. But men are apt to be neglectful about recognizing in others the right of self-determination which they claim for themselves. They impose themselves upon one another and are apt to treat others as means to their ends. And in this manner the rational and moral life is hindered. What could be an advantage to all would be some device which removed or lessened this hindrance. A civil society is, precisely, a device of this kind. It is a device to enable each man to cultivate his own individuality while interfering as little as possible with a similar activity on the part of every other man. The office of a government is to limit by external laws the freedom of any individual to the extent of its agreement with the freedom of all other individuals. This condition Kant calls a condition of justice; and consequently the office of government is to maintain justice.

A civil society, then, is understood to be an association of individuals who have agreed to set up external rules of conduct and a means of enforcing their observance, designed to mitigate the collisions which are apt to occur between the external activities of individuals each intent upon cultivating his own individuality. And if it is asked, how, by imposing rules of behaviour which manifestly curtail the freedom of those who are obliged to obey them, can the result be a condition of greater freedom?, the answer is: first, the rules are the same for all; secondly, they concern only external acts; and thirdly, by concentrating all the interference which a man may be required to suffer into that imposed by law, he is relieved from the continuous arbitrary uncontrolled interference which he would otherwise be apt to suffer at the hands of his neighbours. Nevertheless, a civil society must be understood only as a serviceable but not infallible device for making easier the rational and moral life. But it is to be recognized as a unique kind of association, differing from all others in not having an end to pursue beyond the maintenance of itself, that is, of the condition of 'justice' which it is designed to procure. All other associations – those concerned with industry or trade, for example – are associations to procure some end beyond their own existence; the end of a civil society, on the other hand, is nothing other than the realization under compulsory laws of the right of each man to choose his own ends by securing him against the arbitrary encroachments and assaults of others. The three rational principles upon which such an association must be founded are: the liberty of every member of the association as a man; the equality of every member as a subject; and the individuality of every member as a citizen.

Now, Kant draws from all this one very important conclusion, which he returns to again and again, namely, that the public authority of a civil society, the government, has no more right than any individual to impose upon its subjects notions of its own with regard to happiness or the good life. In short, the common good of the association is solely the good enjoyed in having a referee to decide the disputes of individuals, each of whom retains his absolute right to choose for himself the direction in which he shall seek his own happiness.

'The idea of justice', says Kant,

> arises wholly out of the idea of human freedom in the external relations of men to one another. As such, it has nothing specifically to do with the realization of happiness as a purpose which all men naturally have, or with the prescription of the means of attaining it; and it is absolutely necessary that this End should not be confused with the laws of justice as their motive. Justice in general, may be defined as the limitation of the freedom of any individual to the extent of its agreement with the freedom of all other individuals, insofar as this is possible by a law which applies equally to all subjects.

And again, he says:

> In regard to happiness, no principle that could be universally applicable can be laid down for the guidance of legislation; for not only the circumstances of the time, but the very contradictory and ever-changing opinions which men have of what will constitute happiness, make it impossible to lay down any fixed principles regarding it. . . . No one can prescribe for another what he shall find happiness in.

And again:

> No man has the right to compel me to be happy in the peculiar way in which he may think of the well-being of other men; but every man is entitled to seek his own happiness in the way that seems best to him, if it does not infringe the liberty of others in striving after a similar end for themselves when their liberty is capable of consisting with justice.

In short, the office of government is understood to be that of refereeing the activities of its subjects, all of whom remain individuals. It has neither right nor duty of imposing upon its subjects any substantive activities whatever.

One important question remains. To be a member of such an association is clearly an advantage to any man, because all men are liable to suffer interference from others; but how could such an association be constituted?

Clearly there are immense difficulties, the most obvious of which is that its rulers will be men who have the same propensity as any other men to treat others as means to their own ends. This fact will naturally make subjects wary of endowing their rulers with so much power that they might be tempted to go beyond the duties of a referee. But in the end it is an insoluble problem; all that can be done is to constitute government in such a manner that it is tempted as little as possible to overstep its office of maintaining justice by means of laws applicable equally to all its subjects.

But the 'idea of reason', as he says, which Kant believes to indicate the manner in which such an association might be constituted, is the idea of a 'compact' or 'agreement' or 'consent'. He will have nothing to do with the notion of an historical, original compact, nor does he involve himself, as Locke does, with the difficult idea of tacit consent. What this notion of agreement or consent or compact signifies to Kant is the principle that a just law is one to which all could concur without jeapordizing the equality of each as an individual subject. If a law be of such a nature that it is *impossible* that all subjects could give their assent to it, then it is, for that reason, unjust.

In Kant's *Rechtslehre* and his other writings on politics, then, there is, I think, to be found a genuinely philosophical version of the political theory of individualism. This might have been illustrated further by considering Kant's theory of propriety and his theory of punishment, but enough has been said to show the direction of his thought. He would, I believe, never have set out on this enterprise if there had not been an unmistakable experience of individuality. His task was to give this experience a metaphysical and ethical context, and he performed it more thoroughly, perhaps, than any other writer. Indeed, I think the only other writers with whom, in this respect, he may properly be compared are Spinoza, Hobbes and Fichte.

Adam Smith: Rules and Justice

I propose to spend the rest of this lecture considering two explorations of the political theory of individualism by two writers who owed much to one another intellectually but whose versions of the theory have characteristic differences: Adam Smith and Edmund Burke.

Adam Smith is, of course, renowned as an economist and as the author of the *Wealth of Nations* (1776); but besides this work, which itself is concerned as much with public policy as with economic theory, he wrote two others which have a direct bearing on our subject: *The Theory of Moral Sentiments* (1759) and *Lectures on Justice, Police, Revenue and Arms* (1763). We may look in his writings for a treatment both of the theory of individuality and of the theory of the office of government consistent with individuality.

As Adam Smith understands it, each human being is, in the first place, concerned with himself, with his own desires, aspirations, enterprises and fortunes. This he takes to be an observation. And he believes, also, that it is quite right that men should be concerned with themselves; or at least there is no point in disapproving of this characteristic, for to disapprove of it would be to disapprove of human nature. This is not a very philosophical elucidation of the situation, but it serves Adam Smith as his starting-point. He begins with individuals intent upon making choices for themselves.

But further, it may be observed that men lead more profitable lives, enjoy a wider range of more easily satisfied choices, when they associate and help to supply each other's wants. For, in general, every man desires not merely to obtain the humble necessities of life (food, clothing and lodging), but to procure these according to his own individual taste and specification. Indeed, the whole of current human industry is engaged in procuring not necessities, but opulence. And since opulence springs from the division of labour, and the division of labour from the propensity of men to barter with one another, they will get what they seek only when they associate with one another.

Men, therefore, are individuals, each with tastes of his own, who stand in need of the assistance of others in order to satisfy their numerous and diverse desires. Utility drives them to associate with one another: 'self-love is the impulse from which we save one another'. Moreover, there is a disposition in human nature which underwrites utility in this matter and also extends the range of our moral sentiments: the disposition to take a sympathetic interest in the fortunes of others. Of course, we may be expected to have a readier sympathy for those who are close to us than for those who are distant; but what confirms us in the belief that this sympathy for others is genuine is the observation that we are reassured and even delighted when we find our own feelings and judgements supported by the feelings and judgements of others. And in this feeling of sympathy we come to understand 'that we are but one of a multitude, in no respect better than any other in it; and that when we prefer ourselves so shamefully and blindly to others, we become the proper objects of resentment, abhorrence and execration'. In short, we not only recognize ourselves as natural individuals, moved by our own desires, but recognize others as also of the same character as ourselves, and that in consequence they have a claim upon our consideration. 'The man of the most perfect virtue, the man whom we naturally love and revere the most, is he who joins, to the most perfect command of his own original and selfish feelings, the most exquisite sensibility both to the original and sympathetic feelings of others.'

You will observe what Adam Smith has done, and how he has done it. He has moved from man as an individual with a disposition to explore and enjoy his individuality, to man as an individual recognizing a like character in all other men; and the mediation of this change is the empirical observation of a disposition of sympathy in all men. In short, he has done rather clumsily and empirically what Kant did economically and logically.

Now, continues Adam Smith, if natural beneficence were as strong a disposition as self-love, we should, no doubt, always go to another man's assistance out of friendship, generosity, sympathy and good will. But it is not. And further, it does not need to be in order for there to be associations of men supplying each other's needs and procuring opulence for one another. What is required for an association is not mutual love and good will (though these, no doubt, are an advantage), but merely a disposition not to injure one another – which is something very much less than good will. 'Society may subsist among different men ... from a sense of its utility, without any mutual love and affection ... society, however, cannot subsist among those who are at all times ready to hurt and injure one another.' A disposition not to injure one another is, then, the real foundation of an association of men, and this disposition Adam Smith calls 'justice'.

'Justice', then, is not a readiness to love, but a readiness to refrain from doing injury. But although no association can subsist without 'justice', we do not think that we ought to behave justly because otherwise society would fall apart, but because justice is due to every man as an individual; societies are never more than associations of individuals, and 'justice' is care for individuality. We are no more concerned, says Adam Smith, with injury to a single man because he is a member of a society and because in this injury to him the society itself may suffer injury, than we are concerned for the loss of a single guinea because this guinea is part of a thousand guineas and we should be concerned for the loss of the whole sum. 'In neither case does our regard for the individuals arise from our regard for the multitude; but in both cases our regard for the multitude is compounded and made up of the particular regards we feel for the different individuals of which it is composed.'

The counterpart of 'justice' is punishment and redress for injuries done and suffered. To think of an action as 'unjust' entails approving of its being forcibly obstructed or punished. We do not regard the absence of friendliness or of good will or of generosity as meriting punishment, because it is not an injury. There are certainly praiseworthy dispositions, but their absence does not call for redress because it is not an 'injustice'. Moreover, our concern for 'justice' is not merely limited to those whom we regard as admirable characters; we do not think a man should have to suffer injury unredressed because we disapprove of his character in general. The only relevant question in 'justice' is, has an actual injury been suffered by a specific person? In other words, from the point of view of 'justice' and of the subsistence of an association, a man is an individual capable of suffering and of causing injuries. To be a person is to have a 'natural right' not to be made to suffer these injuries, and a natural duty not to cause them. And the injuries in question may be bodily injuries, may be a deprivation of freedom of movement or choice, or they may be injuries to credit, to reputation or to property. The right to 'justice' is thus the right, not to the good will of others, but merely not to have one's person or property invaded.

Here, then, is Adam Smith's theory of individuality, and his understanding of the office of government is its exact counterpart. The office of government is to provide the conditions of justice for its subjects. It is not to make its subjects 'good' or friendly or generous to one another, but to see that they behave justly to one another, that is, to see that the injuries they do to one another are redressed and punished.

In the first place, then, a government has two duties to perform. First, it must make rules of conduct in which the injuries that men are apt to do to one another are recognized, and to keep these rules of conduct up-to-date. New activities will produce new opportunities of doing and suffering injury, and these should be recognized in the current rules of conduct with as little delay as possible. And secondly, it must provide judges and a judicial procedure to redress and punish injuries suffered or done. 'To prevent the confusion which would attend upon every man's doing justice to himself, the magistrate undertakes to do justice to all and promises to hear and to redress every complaint of injury.' And this is both useful and possible only because 'justice is the only virtue with regard to which exact rules can properly be given'. 'The rules of justice', he says, 'may be compared to the rules of grammar.' They are 'precise, accurate and indispensable'. The rules of the other virtues are comparable to the precepts of literary critics 'for the attainment of what is sublime and elegant in composition', which are 'loose, vague, and indeterminate, and present us rather with a general idea of the perfection we ought to aim at, than afford us any certain or infallible directions for acquiring it'. In short, 'justice' is susceptible to precise rules, and is impossible without a referee. It is the first office of government to provide these rules and to act as this referee. And what induces our loyalty and obedience to government is 'utility' – that is, the recognition that even if, in its imperfection, it does not always provide one with the exact redress I seek, yet it does so by and large – and 'authority', that is, the natural submissiveness we have to men of superior insight into the conditions of justice appropriate to current beliefs and activities.

There are, however, two other duties connected with the office of government. First, since all men desire opulence, and since opulence is the product of the division of labour and the exchange of goods and services, it is the duty of government to provide a stable means of exchange, namely, a reliable coinage, and to refrain from raising revenue for defraying the costs of government in manners hostile to opulence, namely, the sale of monopolies and special privileges and taxes on industry and enterprise. And secondly, since both justice and opulence at home are liable to be invaded and destroyed by the activities of other foreign associations, it is the duty of government to provide for the defence of the association against its enemies abroad. But always there is the dilemma, which can never be finally escaped from: if the government is weak in providing justice, nobody will be industrious and prosperity will suffer; but if the government is strong in providing justice, its command over the association will be apt to provoke it to engage in impoverishing wars.

Adam Smith's contribution to the political theory of individualism is, then, not without some subtlety. It springs unmistakably from the empirical observation of the disposition to be an individual, and it tries to find a theoretical foundation, or justification, for this disposition and to elicit the office of government appropriate to it. If it has a theoretical fault, perhaps it is that he is not very economical in the number of hypotheses he calls into use.

Burke: Government as a Restraint on Passion

Edmund Burke is best known in respect of his views about the proper constitution of government and its title to exercise authority. His main criticism of the theories and practices of the Jacobins, for example, was that they seemed to suppose that because each man has a 'natural right' to govern himself and to secure justice for himself, he must therefore have a civil right to share equally with every other man the activity of ruling a civil association. Burke understood this Jacobin view of things to be muddled and unsatisfactory because it was not only subversive of all existing governments but was also destructive in principle of all civil authority whatever, including that of the Jacobins themselves. It was, as he understood it, a muddled doctrine of anarchy. And it was in respect of his views on this topic that he was selected as an opponent by Tom Paine.

But, in addition to his theory of the proper constitution and activity of governments, Burke has other less well-known views about the proper office of government, and in respect of these Tom Paine, if he had attended to them, would have had little to quarrel with. It is with Burke's views as the proper office of government that we are now concerned.

Like some other contemporary exponents of a political theory of individualism, Burke's theory of individuality is cast in the form of a theory of the natural rights of man: the questions he asks are similar to those asked by Locke, by Kant and by Adam Smith, but his answer is in a different idiom from theirs.

With Burke we begin, then, with individual human beings who have a right to make choices for themselves, a right to exercise their individuality. And the transference from the proposition *this is what men are like*, to the proposition *this is how they ought to behave*, is made in the perception that *this is how God created them, this is the precept of the moral Law of Nature*. And, following the contemporary convention, Burke understands the natural right to be and remain an individual as the natural right to 'self-preservation', that is, to defend himself against any abridgement by another individual of his activity of self-determination.

> The fury which arises in men's minds, on being stripped of their goods and turned out of their houses by acts of power, and our sympathy with them under such wrongs, are feelings implanted in us by our Creator, to be (under the direction of his Laws) the means of our preservation ... they arise out of instinctive principles of self-defence and are executive powers under the legislation of nature, enforcing its first laws.

Now, the expression 'and our sympathy with them', in this passage, indicates the manner in which Burke proposes to turn a natural disposition into a moral disposition. The individual with the right to assert this individuality while denying a similar right to all other men has no moral existence. The natural right to self-determination, as Burke puts it, 'implies a duty' to recognize this right in any other man. Or again: 'Men are never in a state of *total* independence of each other. It is not a condition of our nature.' The real natural rights of man do not represent the individual's pure impulse of self-assertion, but constitute a right of self-assertion in which is recognized the same right in every other man. In short, what for Kant was a piece of illogicality (claiming individuality for oneself and denying it to others), and for Adam Smith a failure to recognize the minute human disposition of 'sympathy', Burke identifies as a moral enormity – the non-recognition of the counterpart duty to the right of self-assertion. But, one way or another, for all these writers, human associations are not inexplicable miracles, they are potential in the individuals who compose them. Nevertheless, Burke, no less than Locke and Kant, but in distinction from Adam Smith, finds the notion of a contract or agreement between individuals, the notion of 'consent', a useful notion with which to indicate that associations are not imposed upon men but are the products of human choice, and that they are unions of individuals, each with his own right and propensity to make choices for himself.

An association of human beings, however, can be discerned to have a utilitarian purpose; and, as Burke understands it, that purpose is, precisely, to provide a ruler or government with authority over its members. This is uniquely true of a political association, a state; this sort of association is a union of individuals who are engaged in a great variety of pursuits and hold a great variety of different moral and religious beliefs, but have in common only this need for government. And the best state is that which finds room for the greatest possible number of different patterns of activity.

What, then, is this activity of governing and this experience of being governed? What human want does it provide for? 'Government', says Burke, 'is a contrivance of human wisdom to provide for humam *wants*. Men have a right that these wants should be provided for by this wisdom. Among these wants is to be reckoned the want, out of civil society, of a sufficient restraint upon their passions.' 'The great use of government is as a restraint.' And the 'passion' that calls for restraint is the passion of self-assertion regardless of the rights of other individuals. What a government provides is rules of conduct for all to follow equally, and an independent judge or umpire with authority to settle disputes between individuals. In other words, we have here a restatement of the Lockean doctrine that the office of government is to assure each man of his natural rights – but Burke does not need to add (as Locke and Adam Smith had to add) 'insofar as they are consistent with the enjoyment by others of their natural rights', because he has already assimilated natural and civil rights to one another in his understanding of a man's natural rights as carrying with them the concomitant duties of mutual recognition. Government is indispensable solely because passionate men are apt not to give this recognition on all occasions, but only when it suits them.

Now, the counterpart of this understanding of the office of government in providing for the restraint of passion is that it cannot and must not be understood to provide anything else. And above all it must not be understood to provide for the 'necessities' of its subjects. In other words, the office of government is not to determine the desires and activities of its subjects, not to settle their condition of life, not to employ them, or to manage them as a team, but to umpire the collisions which are apt to occur between the numerous individuals and teams of individuals, each with their own interests to pursue and each with their own notions of happiness, which compose the association over which it rules.

Burke's version of the political theory of individualism is, then, at least a semi-theological version: like that of earlier writers, his method of generalizing the empirical observation that what we have to deal with is men able and accustomed to make choices for themselves involves attributing this current character of human nature to a divine dispensation. And when he comes to consider the office of government in such circumstances, he formulates it, not in the utilitarian terms of cooperation between men who have need of each other's assistance, but in the more old-fashioned terms of the necessity of restraining the human 'passion' of egoism and self-assertion. And consequently he observes the activities of government springing from (and supported by) not the felt convenience of cooperation, but the government which any man is obliged to exercise over his own passions but which he often fails to exercise.

6

BENTHAM AND MILL

Of all the versions of the political theory of individualism, Bentham's version is that which has the most untidy but at the same time the most elaborate philosophical facade and, nevertheless, is, at bottom, the most pragmatic and empirical. It has been suggested that this untidiness is, to some extent, a designed untidiness; and I myself find this suggestion convincing and fruitful. At all events it is so untidy, so riddled with inconsistencies and half-constructed arguments that the hypothesis that it is, in some respects, intended to be so, is rather more plausible than the hypothesis of total inadvertence on the part of its author. And I would like to take this opportunity of calling your attention to an essay by Mrs Shirley Letwin (*Cambridge Journal*, March 1953) which elaborates this interpretation and to which the view of things I shall put before you now is greatly indebted.

Bentham: The Pre-eminence of Tolerance

Bentham is a 'modernist' in the sense that his main concern is with the proper office of government. He had, it is true (especially in later life), a variety of opinions about the proper constitution of government – or, at least, about the constitutional changes he believed to be desirable in England – and he took some interest in framing constitutions for (for example) the nascent states of South America. In England he came to favour the abolition of the monarchy and of the House of Lords, the secret ballot, female suffrage, parliamentary constituencies of equal size, the election of the Prime Minister by Parliament, and the appointment of civil servants by competitive examination. But Bentham was not a constitutional reformer of a commonplace kind like, for example, Tom Paine. His thoughts did not begin in projects for constitutional change; indeed, there is some evidence that what provoked him to consider constitutional change was the rejection in 1811 of his project for a model prison – the Panopticon. And that his main concern was with the proper office of government is confirmed by the fact that one of the principles which he believed separated him from most of his predecessors was the principle that the duties and engagements of government cannot be derived from the manner in which a government has been constituted or from any beliefs about the derivation of its authority. What, after an early indifference in this respect, he came in the end to believe was that the manner in which a government is composed must play a decisive part in determining its good or ill performance of its office, but that the office itself was based upon other considerations. In short, all, or most, of Bentham's projects for constitutional reform are undisguised inferences from his conclusions about the proper office of government, and their importance lies in the light they shed upon these conclusions.

In constructing his answer to the question, what is the proper office of government?, Bentham may be said to have believed that two main considerations had to be taken into account:

    (a) The character of the subjects of government.

    (b) The character of rulers.

In respect of each of these he was often disposed to state his conclusions in universal terms; he appears to be talking about human nature in general and to think himself to have reached some impugnable, 'scientific' truths about the motives and ends of human conduct. This, however, is the philosophical facade. At bottom he is being empirical and is talking about current human nature and the current probabilities of human conduct.

What sort of people are they who compose the subjects of government? What can we safely say about their beliefs and conduct?

The subjects of government are recognized by Bentham to be sentient and rational beings. Their conduct is determined by a desire for pleasure and an aversion to pain; and each one of them must be supposed to know better than anyone else what in fact is pleasurable and what in fact is painful to himself. Thus, these subjects may be identified as separate, adult individuals, each engaged in making choices for himself, choices which are always determined by the quantity of pleasure and pain believed to be likely to accrue. The notion of self-improvement has no place in the composition of these individuals, and they are incapable of being improved by the activity of one another. What each seeks is merely improved conditions of living in which the preponderance of pleasurable sensations over painful sensations is greater and more certain; and all they can do for one another is to hinder or help each other in the achievement of these conditions. They are engaged in multifarious activities and occupations both competitive and cooperative, and they are apt to entertain a great variety of opinions on every conceivable subject. They live in separate dwellings, and (always in pursuit of pleasure) they are apt to make connections of sympathy with one another such as those which result in marriage and the generation of children. In short, a government must be understood to rule subjects each of whom is primarily concerned with his own condition of life in terms of pleasure and pain, but who are capable of sympathy with one another and even of benevolence towards one another. They compose no 'community' which could be supposed to have an 'interest' or a 'good' of its own. All that there is, is an aggregate of individuals constituted by their 'habit of paying obedience to a person or an assemblage of persons of known and certain description (whom we may call governor or governors)'.

Now the consequence of all this, a consequence of both the selfish and the benevolent propensities of men, is that they are apt to be intolerant of one another's beliefs and activities. This intolerance shows itself in a disposition to subordinate the happiness of others to that of oneself, or to impose upon others one's own beliefs about what constitutes happiness. Indeed, men may even be found banding themselves together (particularly in churches and religious sects) to impose upon all their arbitrary conclusions about good and bad conduct.

Nevertheless, this intolerance is out of place. It conflicts with the principle that every man must be permitted to make his own choices for himself or there can be no happiness in the world; and it generates a situation in which whatever happiness there is, is diminished. For any individual who follows an absolute principle of self-preference unavoidably provokes the opposition of every other individual, and the net result must be to diminish pleasure and to increase pain. And further, self-preference which takes the form of benevolence – that is, the imposition upon others of what I believe to be good for them – is no more defensible than the more naive kind of self-preference, and on the whole it must be considered more pernicious because it can plausibly and insidiously recommend itself as well-intentioned and disinterested.

Bentham, then, like other writers, has come upon a predicament in the human condition. In order to enjoy what nature has fitted men to enjoy, they require a condition not itself supplied by nature. Not to allow each man to make his own choices for himself in respect of pleasure and pain is to deny his character as a sentient and rational being; but when men enjoy this right of making their own choices they are apt to exhibit a disastrous propensity to be intolerant – to disallow in others what they claim for themselves. And from this predicament springs both the need for government and the proper character of government.

Government is a device by means of which conduct which has a tendency to reduce the amount of pleasure available to its subjects is discouraged by having attached to it, artificially, that amount of pain (and no more) which will out-balance the pleasure derived from it by those who pursue it. And conduct which has a tendency to reduce the pleasure available is conduct which has a tendency to make it difficult for men to make their own choices for themselves. In other words, government is a device for making intolerance unprofitable. By means of government we are to obtain from men not good will, sympathy, cooperation or beneficence, but tolerance. 'Tolerance' is, in Bentham's world of ideas, what 'justice' is in that of Adam Smith.

The proper office of government, then, as Bentham understood it, is not to make choices on behalf of its subjects in respect of what is good for them; no man, he believed, is entitled to decide what is good for another sane adult, and nothing is proper in a legislator which is improper in a man. It is not a tutorial or a managerial office; it is not concerned with the improvement of its subjects – indeed, it is not concerned with persons and dispositions at all. What it is concerned with is actions only in respect of their propensity to interfere with the choices of others. In short, the office of government is the office of an umpire who is charged with the duty of neutrality towards all the activities of those whom he rules except in so far as they interfere with one another. 'The principal business of the laws', he says,

> the only business which is evidently and incontestibly necessary, is the preventing of individuals from pursuing their own happiness, by the destruction of a greater portion of the happiness of others. To impose restraints upon the individual for his own welfare, is the business of education, the duty of the old towards the young; of the keeper towards the madman: it is rarely the duty of the legislator towards the people.

It is true, of course, that Bentham sometimes described the office of government as the promotion of 'the greatest happiness of the greatest number'; but, whatever else this expression may mean to Bentham, it did not entail the notion of a happiness superior to, or other than, the happiness which each subject chooses for himself. 'The greatest happiness of the greatest number' is merely what each man may choose for himself, made possible of attainment by being subordinated to the principle of 'tolerance'. And again, although Bentham sometimes speaks of governing as an educational activity, he makes it clear that the education it incidentally supplies (as a by-product of the penalties it imposes) is not an education in happiness, but an education in 'tolerance'. If government makes a positive contribution to the happiness available to be enjoyed by its subjects, it does so not by choosing some superior forms of happiness and imposing them on its subjects, but merely by relieving its subjects of the pressures, benevolent or self-interested, which they are apt to exert upon one another's choices.

Nevertheless, since government is understood in this manner, and since governors are men, and like other men are prone to intolerance, a government apt to fulfil the proper office of government is manifestly difficult to establish and maintain. The power necessary for umpirage is all too easily diverted to the imposition upon their subjects of what rulers themselves believe to be good. And there is no simple escape from this dilemma. Bentham's attitude towards it was practical and, so to say, Platonic. He believed first, that if rulers and subjects alike were brought up to think and talk correctly about the activity of governing, if they were freed from the distraction of fictitious notions such as 'the people', 'the community', 'the common good', 'the public interest' and so on, which suggest that government is concerned with collectivities not wholly composed of separate individuals each pursuing his own happiness in his own way, and that it has some office other than that of mitigating the effects of their intolerance towards one another, there would be less danger of governments' abusing their power either self-interestedly or in the name of benevolence. And secondly, he came to believe that certain constitutional arrangements could be devised which, while not infallible, would make it less easy for rulers to be despotic and impose their own private notions of happiness upon their subjects.

Bentham, then, did not merely wish each man to make his own choices for himself about his own happiness: he believed that the persons he had to do with were, in fact, persons of this kind; and he saw no reason (indeed, no possibility) to change their characters. There is very little that is 'philosophical' about his theory of individuality, and what is 'philosophical' in it is clearly inferior to Kant or even to Adam Smith. But like Kant's moral theory, though for a different and less adequate reason, Bentham's Utilitarianism is almost entirely devoid of substantive moral judgements. His theory of government is exactly tied to what he believed about the character of those who were to be governed; and, consequently, if subjects of another character were to appear – subjects for whom making choices for themselves was no part of their happiness – he would have had to recognize that, in these circumstances, another and a specifically managerial office would inevitably fall to rulers to perform.

J.S. Mill: Between Individualism and Collectivism

It has long been recognized that 'Utilitarianism' is a somewhat misleading expression, that it holds together and generalizes doctrines which in fact are divergent and even incompatible. The so-called 'Utilitarians' had something in common, but it certainly was not a theory of government. And even now the association of John Stuart Mill with Bentham is still a source of misunderstanding; for it is not an exaggeration to say that, both in general and in detail, the tendency of Mill's thoughts on government was in a wholly different direction from those of

Bentham. What Mill believed himself to be doing was to refine the Utilitarianism of Bentham; what in fact he did was to substitute for it an almost entirely different doctrine. Rhetorically, Mill's writings may be said to belong to the political theory of individualism; but substantially they compose a rather muddled and unconfident exploration of the political theory of collectivism. Nevertheless, it is instructive to observe how, under cover of the rhetoric of individualism, Mill shuffled his way towards a collectivist theory of government.

There are, I believe, three tolerably distinct theories of government to be found in Mill's writings. Two of them are formal, and in varying degrees genuinely individualist; but the third is substantial, and, although its starting-place is individualist, it collapses into collectivism.

(a) In the period of his life when he was disposed to be critical of Bentham, Mill's chief complaint was that Bentham, having dismissed 'the community' as a 'fictitious entity' whose reality consists entirely in individual persons, proceeded to reduce these individual persons to the quantities of pain and pleasure they suffer or enjoy. This view of things Mill believes to be erroneous because it finds no room for a qualitative distinction between different pleasures and pains, and consequently excludes the possibility of a man's being motivated by an idea of 'spiritual perfection' – that is, the pursuit of more valuable kinds of pleasures. A man, as Bentham understood him, might improve his circumstances by coming to enjoy a greater quantity of pleasure and a lesser quantity of pain; but the expression 'self-improvement' was meaningless.

Mill, on the other hand, was most concerned to assert the possibility of 'self-improvement': the individual whom he takes as his starting-point is a person able to observe qualitative differences between pleasures and pains, capable of choosing and pursuing more valuable pleasures in preference to less valuable pleasures, and whose well-being consists in doing so. And Mill (in the line of thought we are now considering) argued from this to what he called 'the principle of individuality' or 'the principle of the sovereignty of the individual'; for, in this matter of self-improvement, each man must be regarded as an end in himself and to have an absolute right to make his own choices for himself. Indeed, Mill's ideal man is essentially an active and energetic character, intent upon improving not only his circumstances, but also himself.

The principle of individuality, then, entails, for Mill, 'liberty and spontaneity'. And in this mood he is disposed to recognize an absolute value in the 'self-direction' a man may exercise over his own activities whatever they may be, or, as he calls it, 'eccentricity'. Unless this individual is recognized to be genuinely sovereign over himself, the spring of 'self-improvement' will be absent, and society will degenerate into an inert and ossified condition.

Nevertheless, men are apt to be negligent in recognizing the 'individuality' of others and are prone to impose upon others their own notions of well-being; hence the need for government, the office of which is to provide a general protection for the enjoyment and exercise of 'individuality'. And hence Mill's suspicion of 'democracy', which he feared might easily assume the office of imposing upon all merely the notions of well-being common to the majority: 'the tyranny of a collective mediocrity' taking the place of the local and partial tyrannies in which the strong oppress the weak.

So far, then, we have from Mill a largely formal account of individuality and the office of government which corresponds to it. Nothing has been said about what in fact are the more valuable pleasures; and government is regarded merely as the protector of each man's rightful sovereignty over himself, the guardian of 'eccentricity'. And, so far, we may be said to have been given a modified Benthamism. But it ends in our impasse: democracy of some sort is the only kind of government appropriate to such individuals, but democracy is fatally liable to use public power to destroy the exercise and enjoyment of individuality. 'The people may desire to oppress a part of their number.'

(b) From this we pass to Mill's second theory of government which, in a sense, may be said to be designed to rescue us from this impasse. Since government cannot be relied upon to guard the sovereignty of an individual over himself, a limit must be set to its authority, thus minimizing the damage it may do. Under whatever political institutions we live, there is a circle round every individual human being which no government, be it that of one, of a few, or of the many, ought to be permitted to overstep. And Mill expounds the principle of this limit in terms of a distinction between 'self-regarding' and 'other-regarding' actions. 'The only part of the conduct of anybody, for which he is amenable to society, is that which concerns others. In the part which merely concerns himself his independence is of right absolute. Over himself, over his own body and mind, the individual is sovereign.'

Leaving on one side the impossibility of operating this distinction, but noticing that the distinction itself is as wholly foreign to Benthamism as the qualitative distinction between different pleasures and pains, what Mill offers us here is a fresh understanding of the office of government. A man's individuality, we must suppose, is exercised both in his 'self-regarding' and in his 'other-regarding' activities. In respect of his 'self-regarding' activities government has absolutely nothing to do; they are wholly insulated from its attentions. It is concerned solely with his 'other-regarding' activities – his activities insofar as they affect other people. But what is its office in respect of these activities?

Mill's answer to this is remarkably indefinite, but one thing is clear: having insulated at best part of the sovereign individual from the attentions of government, he can afford to take a more generous view of the proper office of government in respect of what remains – that is, 'other-regarding' actions. His view remains largely formal: the proper principle of government is to protect the exercise and enjoyment of individuality, but there is no specification of the conduct to be enforced except the duty to respect individuality in others. Nevertheless the way has been opened for a new line of thought to intrude itself – a line of thought turned away from any kind of genuine individualism. Indeed, each of Mill's departures from Benthamism may be recognized as an often inadvertent step in the direction of a collectivist theory. The contention that certain kinds of pleasure are more valuable than others led to the recognition of certain kinds of people as more valuable than others, and with this the foundation of Bentham's principle of toleration was undermined instead of being reinforced. The formality of Mill's notion of 'self-improvement' invited the intrusion of notions which would deprive it of its individualist basis. Mill may assert the absolute value of 'liberty', 'spontaneity', 'diversity' and 'eccentricity', but the assertion is left hanging in the air. In short, what we are waiting for is the reasoning which will make these assertions intelligible; and when we get it, it turns out to be a theory in the collectivist idiom.

(c) One of the beliefs with which Mill left Benthamism behind was his belief in progress and the ultimate perfectability of mankind. He shared with some of his contemporaries a belief that the history of the human race should be regarded as a unilinear advance in which an ever higher degree of civilization gradually established itself, an advance which would terminate in a condition recognized to be perfect. And it is in terms of this belief that he came, in the end, to construe his convictions about the value of independence, and the importance of preserving diversity and eccentricity. He had no absolute objection to uniformity; he believed that in the end true opinions would establish themselves and that there was a single condition of well-being appropriate to all men. What he objected to was uniformity, the suppression of opinion and of individual efforts at self-improvement at the present time. For he understood the progress of mankind to be achieved by experiment, and the growing-point of progress was the efforts of independent and thoughtful individuals to improve themselves. In the final analysis, the individual for Mill is not an end in himself: he is an instrument and a servant of racial progress. His sovereignty over himself is the counterpart, not of his character, but of his present condition of ignorance and uncertainty, Mill's plea for diversity is methodological, not substantial: diversity must be allowed only because we cannot yet be certain about what is true and what is false. But he looks forward to a time when the uniformity of perfection will establish itself unmistakably. For example, when Mill gives his reasons for believing in the importance of allowing the freest possible play of opinion in a society and of tolerating heterodox views, he is not concerned with the right of the individual to hold whatever opinions his thinking has led him to, but with the duty of the individual to participate in what he understands to be the age-long debate in which 'truth' will finally emerge. They are the reasons which Milton had used two centuries earlier.

In short, 'individuality', 'diversity' of opinion and 'eccentricity' of behaviour are all understood by Mill as the means by which a final condition of 'truth' and 'well-being' would be established. The rights of individuality are not absolute, but temporary and conditional. And when Mill speaks of education, it is not the education in toleration which was characteristic of Bentham and which belongs to a genuinely individualist theory: it is an education in which people, learning from one another and from the clash of opinion, will gradually replace false ideas by true ideas. The two reasons why current opinions ought never to be suppressed are: (a) that they may be true, and whether they are true or not only the future can reveal, and (b) that it is important that people should find out the truth for themselves and not have it imposed upon them.

With this radical modification of the Benthamite theory of individuality went an appropriate understanding of the office of government. The duty of government is not merely to protect the invasion of one individuality by another, but to assist the current efforts at 'self-improvement'. Some individuals are further on the way to perfection than others, and (although they should not be allowed to impose their views upon their inferiors) they are the proper rulers of mankind; at least their views should be allowed to carry extra weight. And wherever there is expert knowledge it should be recognized in government. Mill, of course, is very far, as we shall see later, from any conception of the rule of the Saints; but his peculiar theory of individuality in the end left him looking in that direction. His last thoughts on government are bureaucratic rather than democratic. He understood mankind to be engaged in a cooperative enterprise to discover the true character of human well-being; and he understood government to have a part to play in organizing and controlling the pursuit of this enterprise. And it was only when collectivism spelt 'collective mediocrity' that he feared and disapproved of it.

There is no time to pursue further this history of the political theory of individualism. I have had to leave a great deal unnoticed, and in particular I have said nothing about the contemporary version of the theory which has been elaborated by Catholic (particularly Thomist) writers. But contemporary versions of this theory exist in considerable variety and will be familiar to you. They do not, I think, add anything fundamentally new to what has already been said; but our study of the history of this theory should have shown us that the theory is capable of improvement. And the improvement I would most like to see would spring from a closer attention to what in fact a political theory is, and from a more economical statement of the necessary principles of individualism in this connection.

I believe it to be a virtue in any theory that it avoids calling upon unnecessary hypotheses. And if this is so we are likely to conclude that many of the versions of the political theory of individualism are capable of improvement in this respect. Writers in this idiom, in order to make their position impregnable, have been accustomed to construct a foundation far in excess of what is required to carry the superstructure. They have invoked metaphysical theories of personality, they have appealed to principles of natural law, they have elaborated theories of human nature in general. But what they have written in this respect is not so much erroneous – indeed, it may all be demonstrably true – as unnecessary. And this redundance would, I think, have more clearly appeared if the general character of a political theory had been more fully appreciated.

The political theory of individualism should, I think, be understood as the elucidation of a view of the office of government appropriate to certain circumstances. And the chief feature of these circumstances is the appearance of subjects who desire to make choices for themselves, who find happiness in doing so and who are frustrated in having choices imposed upon them. In order to begin to think about the manner of governing appropriate in these circumstances we do not need to demonstrate that a disposition of this sort has eternal validity, that it represents the fundamental structure of human nature, or that no other disposition is conceivable; all we need do is to recognize the appearance of such subjects – namely, subjects intent upon the enjoyment of individuality – in sufficient numbers to make it appropriate to consider the corresponding office of government. What has to be elucidated is not an eternally valid notion of government, but a notion of government appropriate to subjects of this sort. And we require for our starting-place nothing more than the recognition of the existence of subjects of this sort. We know well enough that this is an acquired disposition, we know that there have been communities of men from which it was absent or in which it was relatively insignificant; and we know that such communities may re-emerge. But all this offers no hindrance to the elucidation of the political theory of individualism. All that could make such a political theory unintelligible would be the demonstration that subjects of this disposition have never existed; and all that could make such a political theory of merely historic interest would be the recognition that subjects of this sort do not now exist. And neither of these propositions is capable of being made convincing or even plausible. If we had no other evidence, I consider the undeniable fact that a large part of the intellectual energy of European thinkers over a period of four centuries has been engaged in elucidating a theory of government appropriate to subjects of this character, is evidence enough for our purpose.

In short, the vice of those who have elaborated the historic versions of the political theory of individualism is that they have tended to encourage us to expect too much from their reflections. And the best of the writers in this idiom are, I think, those who have pitched their expectations low, that is, those who have not lost sight of the fact that what they were doing is no more than exploring a theory of government appropriate to certain historical circumstances.

The same conclusion appears, I think, if we look at the situation from the opposite direction. What these writers had before them was a current manner of governing – that is, governments which were apt to behave in certain ways and to interpret their office in a certain manner. And the political theorist could ask himself what were the entailments of this manner and notion of government. Here, again, he might be over-elaborate, he might go further than was necessary for the explanation of what he had before him. He might conclude that for governments to behave in this way entailed the existence of a Law of Nature which commanded the recognition of sacrosanct individuals, or the existence of individuals solipsistically separated from one another, or 'human nature' of a certain general character. But if he knew his business he would be on his guard against unnecessary hypotheses. And I believe that any hypothesis is unnecessary which goes beyond the simple recognition of subjects who have acquired (perhaps only temporarily) a disposition to make choices for themselves and to find happiness in doing so; subjects, that is, who have acquired, and are intent upon exercising, a high degree of individuality.

But further, a political theorist who approaches the matter from this direction (that is, one whose enquiry is aimed at elucidating the entailments of a current and obscure manner of governing) would be obliged to recognize that the elaboration of a political theory of individualism would constitute only one half of his task. For the manner of governing which has established itself in Western Europe and America during the last four and a half centuries becomes intelligible only when, in addition to subjects intent upon making choices for themselves, recognition is given to the existence of subjects incapable or unwilling to make choices for themselves. In short, if we are to have a theory that recognizes all that has been afoot in government we must supplement the political theory of individualism with the political theory of collectivism. And I propose next to say something of the history of this idiom of political reflection.

PART III

THE POLITICAL THEORY
OF COLLECTIVISM

7

THE RELIGIOUS VERSION

Although I have devoted considerable space to an examination of the political theory of individualism there is still much that might have been said that I have had to leave unsaid. But it is time now to consider the other main stream of political reflection in modern Europe, namely that which has been devoted to the elucidation of what I have called the political theory of collectivism.

By the politics of collectivism I mean an understanding of government in which its proper office is believed to be the imposition upon its subjects of a single pattern of conduct, organizing all their activities in such a manner that they conform to this pattern. It understands governing as the activity of creating a 'community' by determining a 'common good' and enforcing conformity to it. And the 'common good' concerned is not understood in terms of tolerating the activities and choices of the individuals who compose the society, but as a comprehensive pattern of conduct imposed on all subjects alike.

This, clearly, is a style and understanding of governing appropriate, not to those who valued and enjoyed the experience of individuality, the experience of making choices for themselves, but to those who, for one reason or another, were unable or unwilling to embrace the opportunities of individuality which the dissolution of the communal order of the Middle Ages offered, and who wished choices to be made on their behalf.

This inability to make choices generated a morality of 'solidarity' in which the experience of individuality was recognized as evil. This morality had a deceptive similarity to the old morality of communal ties; but we may escape being deceived by this similarity if we understand that the morality of collectivism is not merely a successor to the morality of communal ties but is also a response to, a reaction to, the current dominance of the morality of individuality. It is the attempt, on the part of those who are unwilling or unable to make choices for themselves, to relieve themselves of the feeling of insufficiency and guilt which, in a world dominated by individuality, this inability generated.

Here, then, was a moral disposition, generated by the circumstances of the early years of modern European history and corresponding understanding of the proper office of government. The situation to which this understanding of government has to be related may be described in this manner.

The world in which I find myself is dominated by people engaged in a great variety of activities, people eager to embrace the experience of individuality, eager to make choices for themselves about what they shall do and what they shall think and believe, and people, therefore, averse to the interference of authority, which they regard, not as the manager and director of their lives and activities, but as the umpire of the collisions in which their activities are sometimes involved. But, by reason of temperamental or circumstantial incapacity, on account of poverty, weakness or misfortune, I find myself unable to share this enterprising life that is afoot. The collapse of the communal order has left me, not eager to exploit the opportunities of individuality, but lost, unprotected, leaderless and homeless. I have been deprived of the sense of belonging to a community but I have neither the intellectual nor the material resources to set up on my own. In these circumstances I come to understand the morality of individualism (which I cannot share) as a form of immorality; and I come to understand the view of government which corresponds with it as a false or inadequate view. The only escape seems to be to a morality which recognizes a 'common good' or a 'communal good' to which my activity and that of all others is subordinated, and to an understanding of government as the custodian and promoter of this 'common good'.

But this 'common good', this condition of human circumstance which it is thought proper to impose upon the association, is not 'given' (as it was in the communal life of a medieval village, for example): it has to be chosen and established. It entails a criticism and a modification of the multiplicity of activities and beliefs which are afoot. And this circumstance carries with it two consequences. First, it means that the condition of human circumstance chosen to be imposed is preferred above all other possible conditions of human circumstance: it is believed to be at least the emblem of a 'perfect' manner of human existence. Government is recognized as the activity of imposing what is believed to be a 'perfect' way of living upon its subjects. And secondly, it means that the office of government is twofold: (a) To determine, to choose the pattern of activities, the condition of human circumstance to be imposed upon its subjects, to choose the 'common good'; and (b) To be the custodian of that 'common good', organizing the activities of its subjects so that each shall make a specific contribution to the achievement of the condition of human circumstance believed to be 'good'.

Now, long before this understanding of the proper office of government displayed itself in the idiom of general ideas, it appeared as a disposition to demand from rulers a style of governing of this character. Subjects who were unable to participate in the experience of individuality looked to their governments for protection from the consequences of the dissolution of the communal life of the Middle Ages; subjects who found themselves dispossessed of their religious faith, looked to their governments to choose for them a new religious faith. In short, the politics of collectivism appeared first, not as a concept of the proper office of government, but as a demand that governments should extend their activities beyond those of an umpire on behalf of those who needed specific protection and help. The Elizabethan Poor Law represented activity of this kind – assistance to those who were unable to fend for themselves. And it only became an understanding of the proper office of government when it was believed that government ought to undertake, not only the management of the interests of those who were unable to look after their own interests, but also the imposition of a pattern of life which should embrace all subjects alike.

One further preliminary observation must be made. We have seen that the aspirations of individuality called for sovereign governments – governments, that is to say, endowed with authority not merely to maintain prescriptive rights but to create new rights. And it is clear that the needs of those who were unable to take the road of individuality called also for governments endowed with sovereign authority; these, no less than their individualistic compatriots, demanded new rights – rights to succour and protection such as no medieval government had had authority to provide. But whereas the aspirations of individuality were inevitably suspicious of governments which were not only sovereign but also exceedingly powerful, the needs of the helpless could be supplied only by governments which were endowed with very great power. And I think it is, generally speaking, time to say that the great access of power which has come to European governments during the last four centuries has been a response, not to the needs of individuality but to the needs of those who have been unable, for one reason or another, to enjoy in any significant degree the experience of individuality.

Now, since, in the politics of collectivism, the office of government is understood to be the imposition upon its subjects of a comprehensive condition of human circumstance recognized to be the 'common good' of the association, the history of the political theory of collectivism appears, from one point of view, as the history of the various patterns of activity which it has been thought proper for governments to impose. Of these there have been a considerable variety during the last four centuries of European history and it would be unprofitable to catalogue them: the differences between many of them are insignificant. But, for the most part, the idioms of 'perfection', so to speak, the conditions of human circumstance believed to represent the 'common good' of an association, may be observed to compose three main versions: first a 'religious' version, where 'perfection' is understood as 'righteousness' or 'moral virtue'; secondly a 'productivist' version, where 'perfection' is understood as a condition of 'prosperity', of 'abundance' or 'wealth'; and thirdly a 'distributionist' version, where 'perfection' is understood as 'security' or 'welfare'. These three versions of the politics of collectivism succeeded one another in the history of modern Europe; but although each (except the last) has declined as its successor mounted in importance, none of them has finally disappeared from the scene. And in our own time the politics of collectivism may be seen to be composed of a mixture in which each of these versions has some place.

The politics of collectivism emerged first in modern Europe in a 'religious' version. Government was understood as the control and management of all the activities of its subjects in such a manner that every activity was made to contribute to a mundane condition of human circumstance denoted by the word 'righteousness'.

The first intimation of this notion of government appeared in the character of the 'godly prince' of the Reformation: a ruler who was recognized to have the office of reforming the Church in his realm, of choosing for his subjects their religious confession, and of making the protection of a Church his first care. The 'godly prince' in, for example, Luther's understanding, was not a genuinely collectivist ruler; his office was limited and specific: it was to establish and protect an ecclesiastical order. Nevertheless, there sprang from this character a genuinely collectivist style of governing, the earliest and most striking example of which appeared in the political theory of Calvinism and in the government of the Geneva of Calvin and Beza, where the activity of establishing and protecting an ecclesiastical order extended itself into the total management of the lives and activities of its subjects.

The design of Calvin, an immigrant refugee from France, was to impose upon the citizens of Geneva an exclusive and comprehensive pattern of activities from which no divergence was to be allowed. This regime was established in 1541. It lasted under his direction for twenty-three years, and it continued after his death with scarcely abated impetus, so that even two centuries later it exercised its influence upon Rousseau.

The activity of governing was carried out by councils of lay elders, advised by a consistory of ecclesiastical colleagues both in what was commanded and in the manner in which it was enforced. The subjects, the citizens of Geneva, were regarded as a congregation whose conduct was to be managed in the minutest detail by an inquisitive and an implacable authority which followed them into their houses, which dictated their food, their drink and their clothing, which directed their work and supervised their play, which managed the education and the conduct of their children – an authority which was indifferent to nothing and punished laxity in conduct, dissidence in speech and error in belief with equal and extreme severity.

The office of government was recognized to be the guardian of God's honour and glory and to be the execution of God's will as displayed in the Scriptures: every divergence or shortcoming in conduct was interpreted as a wilful attack upon God. In this manner a 'city of God' was created whose order was understood to represent righteousness.

Now, what is to be observed is that the Geneva upon which
this regime was imposed was not a medieval community, organized in terms of communal ties, but a supreme example of a
modern community in which its members were 'individuals'
engaged in a great variety of occupations who were apt to
entertain a great variety of beliefs. It was a society in which a
high degree of individuality had established itself, a society in
which eccentricity of belief and practice abounded. It exhibited
no native propensity for the hard and comprehensive discipline
that came to be imposed upon it. And the new crimes which
the Calvinist regime found necessary to institute testify to the
variety of interest, activity and opinion that was afoot. The
pattern, then, was imposed; and it was imposed and main-
tained by force. It was a pattern of life, a 'common good', from
which no person was exempt, not even children. Every subject,
in all his activities, became the agent of a government which
demanded not only obedience and loyalty, but enthusiasm and
gratitude. It was a government which, in the fervour with
which it pursued its chosen idiom of 'perfection', was indisposed to allow mere formalities to stand in the way of achievement. Individuality was suppressed; and for an association
of individuals each intent upon making his own choices for
himself was substituted a collectivist society in which all significant choices were made by its rulers; and the choices they
made, and imposed upon their subjects, were throughout determined by a notion of 'righteousness'.

In the sixteenth century, then, there had already appeared
the notion and the practice of government as the control and
management of all the activities of its subjects: the notion of
government, not as an umpire settling the collisions which
might occur between the activities of individuals, but as the
designer and imposer of a condition of human circumstance
chosen because it was believed to be better than any alternative
condition of human circumstance.

Nor was Geneva a lonely example of this style of governing:
similar regimes were set up in Basel, in Bern and in Zurich,
each of which became a collectivity designed to exhibit a 'perfect' manner of living. The theory upon which these regimes
was based was the belief that the proper occupation of mankind
was to minister to the glory and honour of God, and that all
human activities ought to be subordinated to this purpose.

Another example of this understanding of governing appeared in the aspirations of certain of the sectaries in England

in the seventeenth century, and it is particularly interesting on account of the theoretical construction which went to support it.

In the view of these sectaries, the chief and most important of which were the Fifth Monarchy Men, the office of government was to impose 'holiness' upon its subjects. And the 'holiness' concerned was not a condition of the soul, but a manner of living in this world. This style of governing was called 'the rule of the Saints', and it was made intelligible in an elaborate theory.

The Saints, or the Elect, were understood to be eternally separate from the Reprobate. They were predestined to salvation, and their duty on earth was to rule over the Reprobate. Government was understood to represent the dominion of Grace over Nature, the establishment by force of a 'righteous' community, 'Christ's monarchy on earth'. This was recognized to be a temporary condition to be superseded by the Second Coming of Christ, who would then take the reins of government into his own hands. Meanwhile however, rulers were the agents of God, and their subjects were recognized, not as individuals capable of making choices for themselves, but as members of a collectivity whose sole right was to have a detailed manner of life imposed upon them by government. Sin and crime were approximated to one another, and both were made punishable by government.

Nor did the aspirations of these millenarian sectaries remain mere aspirations: they were reflected in the regime established in England for a period of eighteen years, from 1642 to 1660. That during this period there were more projects than achievements, in Parliament more bills than acts, in the country more acts than enforcements, is no doubt true. But since what we are considering is an understanding of the proper office of government, it is irrelevant. Reflected in the proposals and in the legislation was the view that governing is not an activity of ruling individuals who make their own choices for themselves, but of managing or ordering the lives of subjects so that they compose a pattern of 'righteous' conduct.

Now, the political theory of Calvinism and of the millenarian sects of English puritanism in the seventeenth century are important, not only as examples of the religious version of the political theory of collectivism, but also because they provided the mythology, the view of world history and much of the political vocabulary of the most striking contemporary collectivist theory, namely that of Karl Marx and his associates. We shall observe later that Marxism represents not only the religious version of the political theory of collectivism, but it is appropriate to notice here the manner in which this version penetrated it. Like the millenarian sectaries of the seventeenth century, the Marxist believes that a new age is emerging (a third epoch in world history) in which the dominion of 'earthly' (that is, 'capitalist') governments will be superseded by the rule of the Saints (the proletariat) over the Reprobate (the bourgeoisie), who have no rights save the rights to be ruled and who cannot be 'saved' because they are not among the Elect. In order to prepare for this period of 'Saintly' rule, the Elect (like the Brownists in sixteenth-century England) must separate themselves into congregations which will need a synod to direct their activities. They must claim the right to propagate their beliefs ('the truth') without hindrance, and they will absolve themselves from all promises, contracts, engagements, treaties, oaths and debts. As Butler in the seventeenth century said of the puritan saints:

> ... the godly may allege
> For anything their privilege.

Allies among the Reprobate may be recognized: 'blessed is he who hath any hand in pulling down Babylon'. Any 'cause', however inconsistent with Saintly rule, which serves to shake or embarrass the authority of 'earthly' governments, should be supported: above all the cause of 'freedom' or 'individuality'. When power (an army) becomes available, the claim of the Elect to order their own affairs will be transformed into the assertion of their rights to rule others; and the office of government will be recognized as the imposition of a comprehensive pattern of activities upon all its subjects. Nevertheless, this period of 'Saintly' rule, marked by all the violence and unscrupulousness appropriate to the agents of 'history', and demanding not merely loyalty but gratitude and love, is only an interim between Babylon and the Kingdom of God. From it will spring, at some unspecified date, a 'perfect' condition of human circumstance about which little is known except that there will be no place in it for governing as a specific activity and that it cannot be established anywhere with certainty unless it is established everywhere. In short, there is scarcely anything in the mythology and the anthropology of Marxism which does not have its counterpart in the writings of the seventeenth-century puritan sectaries. The religious version of the politics of collectivism, the first version to appear in modern Europe, has survived almost unchanged (but not, of course, without some additions to it) into our contemporary world in the political theory of Marxism.

Before leaving this version of the political theory of collectivism it is proper to notice the variant of it that appeared in the writings of the eighteenth-century French *philosophes*. The condition of human circumstance to be imposed by government was, for Calvin and the puritan theorists, a condition of 'holiness' or 'righteousness'; for this the *philosophes* substituted 'virtue', but it was a distinction without a difference. The activity of governing was understood to be the creation and maintenance of a 'heavenly city' in which the conduct of every subject would be subordinated to the 'common good'. For Rousseau, the grand question was: what is the character of a government which can make its subjects 'virtuous'?; and by 'virtuous' he meant not merely 'law-abiding' or 'tolerant' or 'just' but 'morally good'. Morelly, Mably, Deschamps, Meslier and other writers of the time all proclaimed a morality in which the sole duty and the sole right was to be an anonymous contributor to the 'public good' of a 'community', in which every man acknowledged himself to be, not an individual pursuing his own ends and with duties to others of his kind, but a 'public man', a servant of the 'common good' – a 'community' in which personal ambition, private property, personal choice were recognized to be evils, and in which 'real' equality was recognized to be the necessary condition of the 'virtuous' life. And the counterpart to this morality was an understanding of government in which its office was recognized to be the creator and custodian of this 'common good'.

But, although these writers owed some of their inspiration to Plato, they were unmistakable pupils of Calvin; their mythology was derived from their puritan predecessors. A new age of virtue, happiness and justice was understood to be at hand, an age when governing was to be the activity of a virtuous elite, or (with Rousseau) of 'the people' regenerated in a magical metamorphosis, and when the proper office of government would be recognized as imposing virtuous conduct upon its subjects. And when the advent of power transformed these dreams (or some of them) into the politics of Jacobinism, what appeared was the religious version of the politics of collectivism in a slightly different idiom. The immediate emphasis was placed upon the unhindered activity of the Elect (the regenerated French nation) in liberating the peoples of the world from their corrupt, incompetent and vicious governments. Jacobinism is Calvinism in the eighteenth-century dress of a rational morality.

We have still to consider the other versions of the political theory of collectivism which have appeared in modern Europe, but before going further it may be convenient to reflect for a moment on what this religious version teaches us about the general character of the theory.

The Political theory of collectivism is an understanding of the proper office of government which is intelligible only in relation to the general character which distinguishes modern European governments. It is a theory which requires rulers to be endowed with sovereign authority and to have at their disposal immense power. Further it takes for granted the character of the subjects of modern governments, namely that they are individuals whose happiness in a great measure consists in the opportunity to make choices for themselves. The enterprise of a government imposing a uniform pattern of activity upon a society is quite unintelligible unless it is recognized that no such uniform pattern exists. And finally, it takes for granted the existence, among its subjects, of people unable or unwilling to make choices for themselves and therefore ready to welcome a government which will impose, not merely upon them but upon all subjects alike, a 'common good'.

Briefly, then, the political theory of collectivism is an understanding of the proper office of government which at once is intelligible in terms of the context of modern European societies (and intelligible *only* in these terms), and is appropriate to a particular class of the subjects of a modern government, namely those who have neither the power nor the desire to make choices for themselves. In short, it entails the suppression of one class in the interests of another class.

But there is another point of view from which this theory may be considered. It entails the belief that there is one occupation proper to mankind, a single pattern of activity which can be identified as the 'good life'. For, in default of this belief the view that it is the proper office of government to choose and to impose a single pattern of activity upon its subjects would be unintelligible. Unless it is believed that there is a single pattern of conduct superior to all others there would be no point in assigning to government the office of choosing and imposing a single pattern of conduct upon its subjects. And yet, as it has turned out, there has been a divergence of opinion in modern Europe about the character of the pattern of activity which may be considered superior to all others and therefore proper to be imposed. So far, we have considered one of the directions which opinion in this matter has taken – namely, the belief that the proper occupation of mankind is to minister to the glory and honour of God, or (in a slightly different idiom) to lead morally good lives. And where opinion has taken this direction, it has been appropriately accompanied by the belief that it is the proper office of government to impose *this* pattern of activity upon its subjects. But, as we shall see, opinion in this matter has taken other directions in addition to this. Briefly, then, from this point of view, the political theory of collectivism is a reading of the proper office of government which requires us to have decided that there is one proper occupation of mankind, a single pattern of activity superior to all others, and to have decided upon the character of that pattern of activity.

How has this decision been made? It is not to be supposed that it has ever been a merely arbitrary decision, a decision exhibiting merely unconditional preference. The proposals that have embedded themselves in the history of the politics of collectivism, have none of them been merely arbitrary inventions: they have all sprung from a conjunction between ancient belief and contemporary circumstance. It cannot be said to be in any way remarkable that this political theory should have emerged in modern Europe first in a religious version; the belief that the proper occupation of mankind is to do the will of God and to minister to his glory was not a new idea to all. All that was new in the sixteenth century was, first, the belief that it was the office of government to force this occupation exclusively upon its subjects, allowing no divergence from it; and secondly, the appearance of governments with authority and power commensurate with this enterprise. And when we turn to the other versions of this political theory, the version in which 'productivity' (the exploitation of the resources of the world) is taken to be the proper occupation of mankind, and the version which gives pre-eminence to 'security' or 'welfare', we may observe that in both cases they are the selection of a current activity, an activity which was already pre-eminent, for exclusive pursuit.

8

THE PRODUCTIVIST AND DISTRIBUTIONIST VERSIONS

We have seen that in what I have called the political theory of collectivism the office of government is to choose and maintain among its subjects a comprehensive pattern of activity. And consequently, different versions of this political theory will be distinguished from one another in respect of the different patterns of activity proposed for imposition by government. We have considered a version of this theory in which the pattern of activity is denoted by such words as 'righteousness', 'holiness', 'moral virtue'. I want now to consider another version, namely that in which the pattern of conduct to be imposed is denoted by the words 'productivity', 'wealth', 'abundance' and so on.

Productivist

Among the activities afoot in the associations which composed sixteenth-century Europe was that in which the natural resources of the world are converted to the use of mankind and made to satisfy human wants. This, of course, does not distinguish sixteenth-century Europe from all other times; this had always been one of the occupations of mankind, pursued with varying degrees of energy and success. But at that time it was being engaged in with a great exuberance of attention and energy. Enterprise was circumventing or pushing aside many of the hindrances, practical and ideological, which had operated to check it or to quallify its success. Here, then, was an activity supremely eligible to be made the centre of a collectivist notion of government; and it cannot surprise us that an understanding of government emerged in which its proper office was regarded as the organization of its subjects for the exploitation of the natural resources of the world. Moreover, this activity was recognized as having the approval of God: the passage in the first chapter of the *Book of Genesis* in which God was said to have given to mankind all the resources of the world, mineral, vegetable and animal, to convert them to their own use, was taken to be the divine authority for engaging in this activity; and the sin of Adam was understood to have done nothing to qualify this gift except to make 'work' a condition of its enjoyment. Thus emerged what I shall call the 'productivist' version of the politics of collectivism: the belief, not merely that men may properly engage in the unlimited exploitation of the natural resources of the world, but that this is so much the pre-eminently proper occupation of mankind that it should be recognized as the pattern of activity proper to be imposed upon a society by its government. This, of course, did not mean that no other activity was proper to be engaged in: it meant that all other activities should be regarded as subordinate and contributory to this activity. Leisure, for example, was permissible; but it was to be regarded as recreation for 'work' and not (in the Aristotelian manner) as the *telos* of 'work'.

The understanding was, then, that a government endowed with sovereign authority and equipped with great power should be recognized as the servant and director of this enterprise, should use its power and activity to impose it upon its subjects, thus not merely promoting human happiness but leading mankind into a future of unparalleled happiness and prosperity.

There was, no doubt, much in sixteenth-century Europe to provoke this view of things, but its first unmistakable appearance was in speculative writers whose imagination far outstripped anything that was yet upon the scene; and incomparably the most important of these writers was Francis Bacon. Indeed, when we consider the place he occupies in the story of the fortunes of this version of the politics of collectivism, it seems appropriate to call it the Baconian version. He did not invent it; but he perceived it with unexampled lucidity and completeness, and every subsequent exponent of this understanding of government has acknowledged his debt to Bacon.

From one point of view, the Baconian view of things comprises three fundamental beliefs.

(a) First, there is the belief that the unlimited exploitation of the natural resources of the world is the supremely proper occupation of mankind, and that nothing in human nature (except idleness and propensity to error) stands in the way of engagement in this enterprise. This belief was not peculiar to Bacon, but he imparted to his own and subsequent generations an excitement and a confidence in relation to this enterprise which was uniquely compelling. He announced the conviction that this is what men ought to be doing, and that this is what they would all do if they threw off the disposition to slothfulness which was the great enemy of progress. He announced, further, a method of research by means of which this activity might be made increasingly fruitful. Indeed, writers of later generations derived from Bacon an almost magic certainty that the necessary knowledge of the natural world would accrue, and power over the natural world and human happiness follow.

(b) Secondly, what Bacon had his eye upon as the proper object of human endeavour was a comprehensive mundane condition of human circumstances characterized by ever-increasing wealth, abundance and prosperity which he regarded as a condition of earthly 'perfection'. He did not believe in a static Utopia; his notion of 'perfect' human circumstances was a condition in which the natural resources of the world were being exploited to the utmost and turned to the use of mankind. He saw no end to this activity; 'perfection' consisted in pursuing it relentlessly, vigorously and to the limit of current knowledge.

(c) Thirdly, Bacon believed that this enterprise must be a cooperative enterprise: enquiry, invention and application alike called for a 'conjunction of labours'. He thought of himself as making a contribution to an undertaking which could be advanced only if it engaged the attention and the energy of every man according to his capacity. Moreover, he anticipated that the enterprise would be seriously compromised if the whole of human endeavour were not focused upon it. In short, he was prompted at once by the capacity he saw in mankind to achieve success in this matter and by the need of a managing director for the enterprise. The *primum mobile* and manager of this enterprise of mundane human 'perfection' he understood to be government.

The office of government, as he understood it, was no less than that of 'settling the condition of the world' – a minute control of all the activities of its subjects designed to convert them to the exclusive pursuit of this 'well-being'. Its business was to promote research, to supervise industry and trade, to regulate prices and consumption, to distribute wealth where it might be most usefully employed, to eradicate idleness and waste, to endow learning and to turn it in the desired technological direction, to settle religion (so that it should not interfere with the enterprise afoot), and to guard the fruits of human energy and invention.

This view of things may be found in any of Bacon's writings, but it is expressed with the greatest simplicity and directness in the fragment called *The New Atlantis*. The public affairs of the fertile and self-sufficient island of Bensalem were focused upon the 'well-being' of its people. Its laws and institutions marked out a definitive direction of activity to be followed exclusively, everything being subordinated to it. Its government emanated from an institution called the House of Solomon, an order or society dedicated to the study and the exploitation of the natural resources of the world. All the glory and magnificence associated with government was centered in the House of Solomon; the heroes of the nation were inventors, scientists, technologists, explorers and industrialists.

In the writings of Francis Bacon then, is to be found the first unmistakable exposition of the political theory of collectivism in its 'productivist' version: understanding of the proper office of government as the manager and director of all the activities of its subjects so that they are concentrated upon the enterprise of exploiting the natural resources of the world in the interests of human happiness. He was followed by a long line of disciples, first in England and later in the continent of Europe, of whom there is time to notice only a few.

In seventeenth-century England perhaps the best example of a writer in the Baconian style is Sir William Petty. Remarkably free from prejudice and profoundly reflective on most matters, Petty was supremely naive in his understanding of the office of government. A state he regarded as a 'circuit of ground', the natural resources of which were available to its inhabitants. He had learned from Hobbes that the 'right' of the ruler was to take sovereign command over his subjects in order to preserve peace among them. But from Bacon he had learned that the proper occupation of mankind was to cooperate in the enterprise of exploiting the natural resources of the world to the utmost, and that the office of rulers was to direct this enterprise. Government, in short, was estate management, and its object was efficient exploitation of the resources of the 'estate'. All conduct should be subordinated to this end, and nothing should be allowed to stand in the way of its uninterrupted pursuit. Religious toleration was to be related, like everything else, to the 'cause' of 'prosperity'; the poor were a regrettably unexploited asset: the power of government should be used to transfer labour from far less to more productive enterprises. The basis of all good government was to be a survey of the resources of the estate, of its natural resources, of the numbers of its inhabitants, of their skills and present engagements.

By the seventeenth century, then, this version of the politics of collectivism had disclosed itself unmistakably. The three beliefs which belong to it were unambiguously displayed: the conviction that the proper occupation of mankind is the exploitation of the natural resources of the world; the conviction that this is an enterprise requiring central management for its success; and the conviction that the proper office of government is to provide this management. And, generally speaking, the subsequent fortunes of this understanding of government reflect the increasing power available to governments – power often generated in connection with war. They reflect an undiminished puritan aversion to idleness and waste; and they reflect an accumulating confidence that 'prosperity' and 'abundance' are the destiny of mankind if human energies are properly and efficiently directed. But the biblical and theological authority for this version of the politics of collectivism, to which Bacon, for example, had appealed, was gradually replaced by the conviction that there is no 'rational' alternative to this view of the proper occupation of mankind, and consequently to this view of the proper office of government.

In England, the visionary and the rationalistic idioms of this version of the politics of collectivism have found a ready supply of partisans since the seventeenth century. The writings of Robert Owen, for example, display both the puritan dispositions of their seventeenth-century counterparts and the industrial achievements and aspirations of the early nineteenth century. Beginning with the wastefulness of poverty and the eligibility of the poor (on account of their helplessness) as candidates for naturalization, the theme of these writings broadens into the enterprise of imposing a single pattern of activity upon all subjects alike, an activity concerned with 'productivity'. Everywhere there is the Baconian certainty that this is the proper road for mankind to follow. Variety of activity and individual choice are, appropriately, abhorred; prevention is preferred to punishment; government is identified with management and education; a millennium of peace and prosperity is announced. The nation is a 'factory'; and the 'perfection' that beckons Owen is the world transformed into the image of New Lanark.

Robert Owen was followed by other writers in England and America and there have been a succession of patrons of this version of the politics of collectivism down to our own day. But it was French rather than English writers who, after Bacon, explored this understanding of government; and in this respect incomparably the most important is Henri de St Simon.

In the writings of St Simon two ideas are pre-eminent. First, the proper occupation of mankind is the relentless exploitation of the natural resources of the world in the interests of human happiness and well-being. The beaver was the king of beasts, an example to mankind. And what in Bacon was a feat of imagination, in St Simon may be observed as common observation: he lived at a time when the fruits of industry which Bacon promised were being harvested. Nevertheless, St Simon considered that the human race had not yet learned the lesson Bacon had sought to teach. It was still idle in this enterprise, easily diverted to other occupations, and (above all) no really serious attempt had been made to organize the resources of a society in a single productive effort. Or rather, there were intimations of such an organization – as, for example, in the military regime of the Napoleonic Wars – but these intimations had never properly been pursued. The poor were still a liability not an asset. For, secondly, St Simon, like Bacon, believed that the productive effort which was to bring happiness to mankind required central direction, and it was the office of government to supply this direction. And, like Bacon, he perceived that this entailed rulers who are technologists. The House of Solomon reappears in St Simon's writings as a governing body divided into three parts: first, a body of scientists, artists and engineers whose business it was annually to plan the industrial engagements of the society; secondly a body of scientists only, who would examine and criticize this programme and control education; and thirdly, a body of industrialists who would carry out the programme. In his picturesque language, St Simon designated government as '*le pape de l'industrie*', whose office was not merely the management of the productive effort of the community by imposing '*un plan général de travaux*' in which all should find employment, but also imposing upon all the morality of solidarity, the morality of '*la classe la plus nombreuse*'. As nearly as possible, individuality was to be expunged from the community in the interests of maximum productivity.

Round this understanding of the proper occupation of mankind and of the office of government, St Simon wove a religion of solidarity and 'sympathy' which he called the New Christianity, and which is interesting because it reflects the perception that with the desuetude of a morality of communal ties, a collectivist 'community' requires for its support a new collectivist morality. And in the main, his most numerous disciples were believers in the St Simonian religion rather than in his political theory. Indeed, it may be said that at the time of his death in 1825 a new version of the politics of collectivism was emerging which was destined to draw into itself the greater part of the collectivist enthusiasm of the nineteenth and twentieth centuries.

Nevertheless, this 'productivist' version has never perished, and, though it has now a strong competitor, it remains one of the most vital components of our political character.

The political theory of collectivism in its productivist version has, of course, a significant place in the writings of Karl Marx, who, like his predecessors, acknowledged the inspiration of Francis Bacon in this connection. The fault of 'capitalism' (or one of its faults) is recognized to be its inefficiency as a method of production; and the fault of *bourgeois* government is identified as its inability to organize the productive enterprise of mankind. Instead of organizing 'abundance', it organizes 'scarcity', and the interest it serves is that of a class, the class of the owners of the means of production, and not that of the society. It is under the inspiration of Karl Marx that the most notable 'productivist' society the world has ever seen has appeared, namely Soviet Russia. Soviet Russia, understood in these terms, is a Baconian society *par excellence*; there is scarcely a feature in *The New Atlantis* which is not reproduced there with an astounding and direct simplicity. And, to some extent (but, as we shall see, not to the exclusion of another version of the politics of collectivism), Russia reimposed upon Europe the ideals and aspirations of a Baconian society. Wherever it is said that what we need is more technologists, wherever it is said that education should be reformed so as to produce greater numbers of scientists, wherever it is said that industrial effort requires central direction in order to achieve the well-being it promises, the voice that speaks is a voice which was first heard in the writings of Francis Bacon, and has never since been silent.

Distributionist

There is, however, a third version of the politics of collectivism which, in some measure, has come to supersede the two earlier versions. It is a product of the nineteenth century, and the pattern of activity in which it finds its vision of perfection is denoted by the words 'security' or 'welfare'. Instead of 'production', its central idea is 'distribution'; instead of an hierarchical society on the Baconian model, ruled by technicians, its central idea is an 'equalitarian' society.

Every version of the politics of collectivism has as its nucleus a notion of 'perfection', a vision of a condition of human circumstance preferable to all others and consequently one to which all human activities should be subordinated, the idea of a pattern of activity which should determine the place and magnitude of every activity. And for the protagonists of this version of the politics of collectivism, the condition of human circumstances denoted by the word 'perfection' is not one in which productive activity is supreme and every other activity subordinated to it, but one in which every member enjoys an equal share of the products of human energy and achievement.

This change of moral outlook, which began to emerge in the early nineteenth century, is clearly related to the circumstances of the time. Its context is a productive activity which has resulted in a remarkable accumulation of wealth, the appearance (or the illusion) of an abundance capable of redistribution. And it emerged first, and understandably, in those parts of Europe where the productive urge had achieved its most remarkable successes – England and France. It did not entail (or it did not immediately entail) a cessation of productive effort; but it did entail a qualification of that effort. Something other than production was to be given first place and was to determine productive and all other activity; and that something else was the equal distribution of the available abundance.

Nevertheless, although what appears in this new scale of

values is a pattern of activity of a new kind, it cannot be said that, in the early nineteenth century, it was an entirely novel notion. What happened then was that, in appropriate circumstances, a moral notion which had always been present in modern European society came to the surface and established itself as a genuine competitor of all other current moral beliefs. In the 'productivist' version of the politics of collectivism, individual choice was to be removed from the activity of production and had been replaced by a cooperative activity directed and managed by a central authority; in the 'distributivist' version, individual choice was to be removed from the activity of distributing the available wealth: the market was to be replaced by a central distributing authority, and the principle of distribution was to be one of 'equality'.

Related to this view of the proper condition of a human society was an understanding of the proper office of government; its office was to establish and maintain this condition of human circumstances, just as in the earlier version the proper office of government was understood to be the establishment and maintenance of a 'body' and of a 'productivist' society. Governments, now unequivocally recognized as sovereign authorities, equipped with great power, were to be given the duty of coordinating all the activities of their subjects in such a manner that each should enjoy an equal share in the wealth available.

The intellectual explanation of this version of the politics of collectivism was in the first place the work of French thinkers, the most notable of whom in the early nineteenth century were Babeuf, Marechal and Buonarotti, the promoters of what they called a *conspiration pour l'égalité*. Their project was to establish what they believed the Revolution to have promised but to have failed to achieve, an *égalité sans mensonge*, and *égalité des faits*. The Revolution was understood to have gone some way to establishing the legal equality of all subjects; what was now sought was 'real' equality – equality of condition. The sole obligation of all subjects was to be a contributor to a 'public good', to be a servant of a 'community'; and the sole right of all subjects was to enjoy an equal share in the 'community of goods' produced by the cooperative activity of all subjects. The *conspiration* came to nothing; but it may be recognized as the first appearance of a new version of the politics of collectivism which was to grow in importance as the century proceeded.

These early French writers were followed by economists

whose centre of interest was the distribution of wealth rather than its production, a centre of interest which may be said to distinguish nearly all economic writers after the middle of the nineteenth century from those in the eighteenth century, and for which the expression 'welfare economics' was coined.

Political theorists followed in the steps of these economists, but what is remarkable is the manner in which this version of the politics of collectivism rapidly penetrated the popular mind. In England, after 1867 the new electorate was very little interested in the manner in which government was constituted, and very little interested in freedom, but it was vastly interested in a redistribution of wealth. And this interest has now become predominant in those parts of Europe where there is significant wealth to be redistributed. Guaranteed minimum wages have turned into demands for a guaranteed annual wage; and all the apparatus of the so-called 'welfare state' belongs to a pattern of living which puts 'security' before any other consideration.

In France, in the early nineteenth century, when the current version of the politics of collectivism was the productivist version, writers like Fourier were seeking a way in which 'work', production, might be made atrractive. Fourier himself wished to attach to it the glamour and romance which still belonged to war, and to give workshop leaders the prestige that belonged to Marshals of France. But by 1848 observers detected in France an almost universal desire to devolve upon government all responsibility and to exchange the risks and labour of business for a public salary. The *fonctionaire* was the most envied of persons. Nassau Senior remarks that thousands of workers were deserting employment at which they were getting 4 or 5 francs a day in order to get 30 sous from the *ateliers nationaux*. Bagehot observed the same disposition. And Sorel generalized it by saying that it was the ambition of all 'democrats' not to work.

Nor was this disposition confined to the poorer classes: it penetrated the professions and the higher levels of business and commerce. It is reflected in the vast extension of insurance of all kinds and in the ready acquiescence which a government prepared to fix prices and wages has met.

It is not, however, a version of the politics of collectivism which has been deeply reflected upon: it has never had so simple and confident an exponent as Francis Bacon. And although it has established itself in European politics, it has not succeeded in entirely displacing the 'productivist' version.

May I remind you that what I have been discussing in this final lecture are two versions of the political theory of collectivism which together have established themselves in modern Europe. This is not the whole of the modern European political character; it is merely the collectivist disposition in that character. And this collectivist disposition has succeeded nowhere in entirely displacing the individualist disposition. These two dispositions constitute the poles of the modern European political character.

INDEX

INDEX

INDEX

INDEX

INDEX